Managing external relations in schools

D0420542

The educational environment of the 1990s is characterized by increasing independence for schools in a more competitive climate. This book is intended to be of direct practical help to those involved in ensuring the long-term wellbeing of schools for the benefit of the pupils they educate. Its aim is to provide both an overview of the issues relating to external relations in schools and an insight into the organizational and planning systems that can be applied to dealing with them. In particular it focuses on the overall field of external relations and on its individual facets, ranging from the management of links with the LEA, liaison with parents, and issues in primary/secondary school links to school identity and marketing. The book is divided into four integrated parts which examine approaches to the management of external relations, links with the educational environment, links with the community and the marketing environment.

Managing External Relations in Schools places the new challenges arising from the Education Reform Act and LMS into a broad context, which is much wider than the common concept of public relations and marketing. This will enable teachers and school managers to consider more systematically the management needs of the institution's external links. Each of the contributors is an expert in his or her own field and has written from the perspective of the real challenges and issues facing schools. Ideas on enhancing efficiency and effectiveness in all spheres of external relations underpin the themes in the book.

Nicholas Foskett is Lecturer in Education at the University of Southampton. His career has included experience in teaching and management in schools and higher education, including a period in higher education external relations. His main research interests include externa͏l rela͏tions͏ ͏ and geographical and environme͏ntal e͏ducation.

Leeds Metropolitan University

17 0142545 0

Educational management series
Edited by Cyril Poster

Managing external relations in schools

A practical guide

Edited by Nicholas Foskett

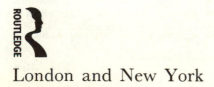

London and New York

LEEDS METROPOLITAN
UNIVERSITY LIBRARY

1701425450

B13CV

373119 26596

371.2 FOS

2 9 MAY 1996 £11.99

First published 1992
by Routledge
11 New Fetter Lane, London EC4P 4EE

Simultaneously published in the USA and Canada
by Routledge
a division of Routledge, Chapman and Hall, Inc.
29 West 35th Street, New York, NY 10001

© 1992 Nicholas Foskett

Phototypeset by Intype, London
Printed and bound in Great Britain by
Biddles Ltd, Guildford and King's Lynn

All rights reserved. No part of this book may be reprinted
or reproduced or utilized in any form or by any electronic,
mechanical or other means, now known or hereafter
invented, including photocopying and recording, or in any
information storage or retrieval system, without permission
in writing from the publishers.

British Library Cataloguing in Publication Data
A catalogue record for this book is
available from the British library
0–415–06833–9Hb
0–415–06834–7Pb

Library of Congress Cataloging in Publication Data
Managing external relations in schools / edited by Nicholas Foskett.
    p.   cm. — (Educational management series)
   Includes bibliographical references and index.
   ISBN 0–415–06833–9 – ISBN 0–415–06834–7 (pbk)
    1. Public relations — Great Britain — Schools. 2. Public relations —
Great Britain — Universities and colleges. 3. Community and school —
Great Britain. 4. Community and college — Great Britain.
I. Foskett, Nicholas, 1955– . II. Series.
LB2847.M36 1992
371.2 — dc20
                                           92–12219
                                             CIP

Contents

Figures

Contributors

Nicholas Foskett is Lecturer in Education at the University of Southampton. His experience includes teaching and management in schools, marketing and external relations management in higher education, and teacher education. His principal interests include teacher education and career development, environmental education and the management of external relations in schools.

Tim Brighouse is Research Machines Professor of Education at the University of Keele, having been Chief Education Officer of Oxfordshire for ten years. Before that he was deputy education officer in the Inner London Education Authority, and worked for various local education authorities in England and Wales. He is an expert in education policy, management and practice, and his recent research projects include school effectiveness and school improvement in an area of inner-city social disadvantage. He has broadcast and written extensively, and acts as an educational consultant to various governments.

Tony Bush is Professor of Educational Management at the University of Leicester. He was formerly a teacher in secondary schools, a professional officer with a local education authority and senior lecturer in educational management at the Open University. His research interests include theories of educational management, school management structures and grant maintained schools. His publications include *Theories of Educational Management* (1986) and *Action and Theory in school management – E325* (1988).

George Campbell is Lecturer in Education at the University of Southampton, in charge of the health, personal and social education field of study. Originally with Price Waterhouse, he has taught in state and independent schools and at Oxford University, and was formerly head of a comprehensive school. His current interests include opening up access to higher education for those men and women who have missed out at an earlier stage in life.

Tony Cobb has been Director of the Regional Staff College, West Midlands, since 1990. Prior to this he had twenty-eight years' experience in five comprehensive schools in Middlesex, Staffordshire and Essex, including sixteen years of headship in two of them. He was a founder member of the Confederation of Coastal Schools, North-East Essex, a pilot exercise in working partnership between schools. His main interest is in school-based INSET for teachers.

Patrick Fullick is Lecturer in Education at the University of Southampton. After working in the oil and gas industry, he became a science teacher and has worked in a number of state schools. His current responsibilities include the training of teachers of science and technology and the provision of continuing education for teachers in these fields, together with the co-ordination of the Enterprise Awareness in Teacher Education (EATE) project in the University. His research interests focus on the ability of formal school education to equip young people with the knowledge and skills needed to live in a complex industrial society. He is joint author of a number of school science textbooks.

Gerry Gorman is Lecturer in Business Studies and Economics at New College, Huddersfield. He is chair of governors of a First School in Bradford, and has wide experience of local voluntary groups. Both have stimulated his interest in fund-raising, and he has worked as a consultant in this field. His publications include *Fund Raising for Schools* (1988) and *School–Industry Links* (1989).

Lynton Gray is Assistant Director (research, information and consultancy) at the Staff College, Bristol. His career has included teaching in schools and a college of education, and the posts of head of the management department, and head of the education management service, at the Polytechnic of East London. His interests in educational marketing have involved him in developing teaching, research and consultancy in the field. He was first chairman of 'The Marketing Network' for those involved in educational marketing, and his publications include *Marketing Education* (1991).

Ina Hanford is Head of Lower School at Walderslade High School for Girls, in Kent. She has held a variety of posts in secondary schools, in both pastoral and academic spheres, and is associate trainer (appraisal) with Kent LEA. Her interests include the management of personnel and staff development in schools, and school–parent links. She writes as both a parent and a senior manager in school.

Michael Ives has been Bursar of Ashville College, Harrogate, since 1978, following a successful career in the Services. His interests include the application of entrepreneurial skills within the educational environment, and his publications include *Promoting Your School* (1990).

John Messer is Headteacher of Christ Church Primary School, in Bradford-on-Avon. He has been a head for more than twenty years, in a small rural school, a large urban junior school, a large infant's school and his current all-age primary school. His interests include the development of pre-school education and the establishment of links between the primary and secondary age phases in schools. His publications include *LMS in Action* (1990) and a training video package, *LMS – The Primary Guide*.

Peter Reader is Public Relations Officer at the University of Southampton, having held PR-related posts in a number of universities and polytechnics. He is a governor of both an 11–16 comprehensive school and an infants' school, and has provided training for governors in Hampshire schools on the management of public relations.

Michael Snell is Principal of Brockenhurst Tertiary College, Hampshire. His career has included work as a lecturer in further education, a period as a further education advisor to Berkshire LEA, and the position of vice principal (marketing) at Bracknell College of Further Education. His publications include *Marketing and Advertising* (1979).

John Watts is a consultant and course director at the Community

Education Development Centre in Coventry. His experience has included the headship of two community schools, and a period as a lecturer at the University of London Institute of Education. His main interest is in the development of community education, and his publications include *The Countesthorpe Experience* (1977) and *Towards an Open School* (1980).

Foreword

Schools and other educational institutions in the public domain are increasingly having to accustom themselves to the necessity of establishing good relations with those outside the profession. The best have been doing this for years: communicating with parents, forging links with other phases of education, involving themselves with the community, working with employers, using the resources of the environment in the widest sense. Now, for many of these activities, there is either legislation or strong pressures that make it essential for all schools to develop their external relations. This symposium, containing as it does a wealth of experience from a wide range of practitioners, is therefore essential reading.

For many teachers the word *marketing* is anathema, calling for bell, book and candle. Certainly there is little relish in the profession for competitive advertising designed to 'sell' a school or college as a superior product. Nevertheless, there is now a growing awareness that the general public not only has a right to know, but also has a contribution to make. To be able to present an institution's achievements in a way that enhances public support is, at a time when the education profession is often under attack for so-called low standards, no bad thing.

As series editor I welcome the addition to the education management series of yet another book that demonstrates both the expertise of its contributors and the practicality of its contributions.

Cyril Poster

Preface

The new era of education that developed through the 1980s and early 1990s has created a shift in both the distribution of responsibilities for managing schools and a changing balance in the nature of the management tasks. In particular, governors have assumed major accountability and the school managerial structure, with its control of devolved budgets, has additional tasks in its portfolio that formerly fell within the remit of LEA officers. Among the new responsibilities, the one that is perhaps most distant from the traditional experience of school senior managers is the sphere of external relations – all those facets of an institution's activities that involve links with the world beyond the school gates. It is a broad field, often mistakenly limited to a consideration of marketing and public relations, in which all school staff play a part. Its efficient and effective management, however, is now more than ever vital to the well-being, and even, in the long term, the continuing survival of the school. Despite this, it is the area in which most new and experienced headteachers, and governors, express concern about their lack of practical experience.

This book examines the new field of external relations management from a practical perspective. It considers the issues, and the strategies and methods that may be deployed to deal with them, in the planning of the whole field of external relations management and within its major sub-areas. The approach is aimed to be relevant to governors, headteachers and senior managers in all maintained and independent schools, from primary to post-16, and is divided into five parts:

PART 1 EXTERNAL RELATIONS IN SCHOOLS – AN INTRODUCTION

The two introductory chapters examine the nature of external relations management issues, and look at both the organization and planning systems that may be appropriate for dealing with them.

PART 2 LINKS WITH THE EDUCATIONAL ENVIRONMENT

The five chapters in this section examine the links that schools have with other parts of the educational world, including links with LEAs, links across the primary/secondary phase 'boundary', and relations with educational support services, further education and higher education.

PART 3 LINKS WITH THE COMMUNITY

This section considers four facets of the school's external relations with the community beyond the educational world. Its prime focus is on links with parents, the media, industry and employers, and the role of the school within the community.

PART 4 THE MARKETING ENVIRONMENT

Part 4 examines the range of activities that are linked to the marketing of the school. It considers the nature of institutional identity, as well as the issues and practice of marketing the school as an educational institution, of marketing the school's facilities, and of fund-raising from outside sources.

PART 5 IN CONCLUSION

In the final chapter, consideration is given to the wider place of external relations issues in education, and the chapter poses some questions and raises issues for the next decade.

Each chapter is written by an author with direct practical experience in the specific fields under consideration. It is hoped that the book will enable those working in and with schools to hone their practice of external relations management in such a way that the quality and value of the educational experience of all the children and young people within schools is enhanced.

Nicholas Foskett

Acknowledgements

The Editor would like to acknowledge the help of the following:

The headteachers of the following schools for granting permission to reproduce their school crests or logos in Figure 12.1:

Burgess Hill School for Girls
Chosen Hill School
Crossley Heath School
Harris City Technology College
Manchester Grammar School
Taunton School
Yateley School

Mary Thomas for her secretarial support
The late Stanley Puttnam, whose support, enthusiasm and ideas were a great stimulus to seeing the project through.

Part 1

External relations in schools
– an introduction

Chapter 1

An introduction to the management of external relations in schools

Nicholas Foskett

The management of external relations has become a central challenge for those working in schools and colleges. At senior level governors and headteachers are recognizing that the long-term well-being of their school or college and its ability to deliver effectively the 'whole education' that is its principal *raison d'être* depend on addressing the issues of the school's relationship with its outside audiences. Issues relating to marketing and image are to be found on the agendas of governors' meetings and senior management team (SMT) meetings with a frequency that would have been unthinkable two decades ago.

There is, however, an unease that quickly emerges when such issues are discussed. Teachers find external liaison an uncomfortable concept, and find contradictions between its apparent objectives and the traditional educational aims. To many, 'external relations' is a term that is synonymous with 'marketing' and 'advertising' and it is regarded as a threat to current practice in education, for reasons identified by Megson and Baber (1986) and Keen and Greenall (1987).

1 It is seen as the intrusion of an alien concept, an idea that has no origin in education, and which traditionally has played no role in it.
2 It is seen as the spread of commercial ideas to the more altruistic world of education.
3 It is seen as a retreat from the school's central focus on teaching.
4 It may be seen as another example of the growth of the 'administrative' function in schools.
5 It is regarded by some as the misuse of scarce financial resources

and the channelling of those resources into non-educational areas.

6 Perhaps most significantly, marketing and public relations are seen as manipulations of the truth and hence both immoral and contradictory to the aims of pedagogy.

These views, however, may be shown to represent some fundamental misconceptions. First, the term 'marketing' encompasses, and has a much wider meaning than, 'selling' and 'advertising'. The Institute of Marketing defines marketing as 'the management function responsible for identifying, anticipating and satisfying customer requirements at a profit'. This profit focus is clearly a perspective from a commercial environment and, while it might apply to some educational institutions in the private sector, it is a view that needs modification for most in education. More appropriate are definitions which emphasize the 'customer' orientation of marketing, for this applies equally in the non-profit-making environment. Two definitions are helpful here:

> Marketing is a complete approach to running a business through focusing all of the company's actions on to the customer.
>
> (Brown 1987: 3)

> The aim of marketing is to know and understand the customer so well that the product or service fits him and sells itself.
>
> (Drucker 1973: 4)

Educational marketing, therefore, concerns itself with the design and delivery of curricula appropriate to the identified needs of individuals or groups. Selling and advertising are usually a part of this process, in that ensuring the customer is aware of the availability of a service is part of the marketing task. Marketing is a carefully managed process that identifies the needs and demands of clients or customers rather than riding roughshod over them. For a service industry such as education it is essential that the dignity of this relationship is maintained at all times, for only through trust, honesty and the pursuit of mutually acceptable goals between the provider (the school), the customer (usually the parent) and the consumer (the pupil or student) can educational objectives be attained.

Second, these views suggest that marketing is the sole element of the institution's relationships with the outside world. Keen and Greenall (1987) consider public relations (PR) in an educational context, and conclude that PR has seven goals in higher education. These are:

1 expanding the number of applicants to the institution;
2 helping the institution to become better known;
3 helping the institution to gain an enhanced reputation;
4 influencing decision-makers to smile upon one's institution;
5 improving internal relations;
6 maintaining good relations with the community; and
7 maintaining productive relations with alumni.

These aims would seem to apply in large measure to schools and colleges, although their relative importance may be different. The importance of recruiting additional students is a clear goal, and this focus of marketing is also of high priority within Devlin's and Knight's list (1990) of the main focus of PR activities in schools. This identifies six target areas for PR activity which a school may wish to prioritize in its own way: marketing; lobbying, to influence political decision-makers; forging and strengthening parent and community links; enhancing links with industry; improving staff recruitment; and making effective and supportive links with the media. All are components of the PR programme that any school may need to introduce, but their importance will vary from time to time and from school to school.

The use of the term 'public relations' so far has been deliberate, as this is the terminology that is most commonly found in the literature and discourse. The Institute of Public Relations defines PR as 'the deliberate, planned and sustained effort to establish and maintain mutual understanding between an organisation and its public'. However, the term may be a little misleading for use in educational institutions, because of its historical link with the commercial world and its negative public connotation of trying to mislead, deceive and create false impressions. More importantly, though, the use of the word 'public' implies a primary focus on existing customers, potential customers and the business's suppliers. The range of audiences is very much wider than this in commerce, but the relative importance of other target audiences in education is so great that the term is misleading. Furthermore, the term suggests that PR is concerned with the creation and management of information flow out of the institution, and is not focused on the management of relationships between many equal partners inside and outside in both a reactive and proactive way.

This idea of partnership characterizes the relationship of schools and colleges with many of their external audiences. It is more appropriate to seek a wider, less jaundiced, term and hence 'external relations' is coming into more widespread use. An appropriate definition of external relations (ER) might, therefore, be:

> Those aspects of an organization's activities that, in any way, cause it to relate to an audience beyond its own boundaries. This includes both processes with an overtly external connection, and those processes which, while largely internal to the organization, have a direct or indirect impact on some external person or organization.

But how does ER management fit into the range of tasks for senior managers? Management tasks at all levels are complex and multifaceted (Torrington and Weightman 1989). The specific tasks to be undertaken vary depending on the time scale and the period of analysis, and Mintzberg (1979) suggests that producing a simple model of management tasks is not easy. In relation to the staff development needs of managers, Ballinger (1986) has proposed a simplified model of management tasks. Ballinger's model demonstrates four distinct spheres of activity: the management of learning, which is the *sine qua non* of educational institutions; the management of human resources; the management of material resources; and the management of external relations. It is clear that such a division is not clear cut. The first three overlap, and all may be said to focus ultimately on the achievement of learning goals. However, the management of external relations transcends the boundaries of the other three spheres in that they all have some external aspects. In addition, it is important to recognize the presence of feedback loops in the system, in that many of the outputs into the external environment, for example, media coverage or examination results, have an immediate inpact on some of the external inputs, for example, recruitment of students or staff, or effectiveness in attracting scarce resources from industrial sponsors.

EXTERNAL RELATIONS – RELATIONS WITH WHOM?

In looking at the nature of external relations management, it is essential to start by considering which groups or individuals constitute the partners with whom a relationship must be established and developed. Devlin and Knight (1990) identify two main target groups for PR: the internal targets and the external targets. The internal targets are in turn divided into the 'immediate school family', including current pupils and staff, and the 'extended school family', covering groups such as parents of pupils. The external targets are also divided into two groups: primary targets, which have an immediate and direct influence upon the school's well-being, such as potential pupils or students and their parents, and secondary targets, whose direct impact upon the school's work is less clear, as, for example, in the recruitment influence of estate agents or priests, or the political influence of the local Member of Parliament. 'Targets' is a term that represents only one facet of external relations work, and a different term that is also of value is 'stakeholders'. This describes those with an interest in the work of the school, and Ballinger (1986) describes four groups of stakeholders: professionals inside education, ranging from teachers to LEA officers and educational psychologists; professionals outside education, including social workers, industrialists and commercial providers of services such as banking and material resource supplies; politically involved individuals, ranging from councillors and education committee members to MPs and individuals with political interests; and consumers of the service. An important distinction that is highly relevant from a marketing perspective is between customers and consumers. In post-compulsory education it may well be that the customer, that is, the individual who makes the decision to 'buy' a particular course, is also the consumer in that he or she will actually attend the course. For schools, however, the two are not synonymous, as the customer is the parent and the consumer is the pupil.

To identify all the stakeholders is a time-consuming, but useful, process. Devlin and Knight (1990) identify which the groups might be from a public relations viewpoint (Figure 1.1). The relationship with each is then a matter for careful consideration, in terms of aims, mutual benefits, management and evaluation, and the aim of this book is to consider the relationship of schools with the principal stakeholders and the processes influencing the development of these relationships.

EXTERNAL RELATIONS – THE RISING PRESSURE

External relations management is a key issue in education. The increasing number of publications in the field, the growth of consultancy work and the linked emergence of specialized conferences and courses are all symptoms of this. What has caused this growth in interest? The simple answer is that legislative developments at national level have created a managerial environment in which external factors come more within the control of senior staff, and where their management may affect the long-term viability of the institution itself. The legislation, however, is also only the product of social and political change over a number of years.

Figure 1.1 Some potential target groups for external relations activities in schools

A For marketing

1. Feeder schools

Local feeder schools, independent and state
Other feeder schools, independent and state

2. Advisors to parents new to the area

Churches

Public libraries

Estate agents
Personnel officers
Local education authority
Citizens advice bureaux
Relocation agencies
HM Forces

B For lobbying

All those listed above plus:
Government
Education committee and chair
Local authority chief executive

Local MPs
Teacher unions
National media

LEA advisors and officials
Local media
Local councillors and committee chairs
District council officials
Local industry

C For enhancing community links

Doctors, dentists and clinics
Churches and clergy
Higher education institutions
Receiver schools and colleges
Community groups
Local shops

Hairdressers
Post offices
Feeder schools
Police
Pubs and clubs
Local media

D Industry links

Careers teachers
Firms employing parents/governors
Work experience co-ordinators

LEA careers service
School supply firms

LEA industry liaison officer

Personnel officers	Chamber of commerce
Local CBI	Local trade unions
Business leaders (local and national)	Business organizations
Company/trade magazines	

E Staff recruitment

Initial teacher training institutions	LEA recruitment office
DFE (Department for Education)	TASC
Organizations providing INSET	Teacher unions
Teacher associations	Educational media
Local media	Nursery schools/playgroups
LEA offices	Personnel officers in local firms

After Devlin and Knight (1990)

The legislative pressure to change reads like a history of educational legislation in the 1980s. The Education Act 1981 was the first step along the path, with its requirement on schools to produce a prospectus for parents of potential pupils. Subsequent legislation – the Education (School Information) Regulations 1981 and the Education (School Curriculum and Related Information) Regulations 1989 – has refined this requirement to include a list of what exactly must be included in this document, although a casual examination of recent prospectuses suggests that schools pay little attention to the detail of the law on this matter. This legislation made schools consider the way in which they communicated with parents, and the nature of the literature they produced. This was further enforced by the Education Act 1986, which introduced the requirement that all schools must hold an annual meeting of parents with the governing body.

Of greatest impact, however, was the Educational Reform Act 1988 (ERA). This enshrined in legislation the idea of parental choice in school selection, creating an educational marketplace for all schools, where before it had only existed in the post-16 sector or in the choice between a state and an independent school. In addition, the introduction of local management of schools (LMS) and the investment of increased responsibilities in governing bodies stimulated change. Schools acquired both the flexibility in spending power that makes them more responsive to the external environment, and the direct responsibility and accountability for their success that make them exercise their managerial skills in this area to the full.

It may be argued that this legislation simply facilitated change that political and social developments made inevitable. Sayer (1989) has considered some of the external changes that have made schools more responsive to their external environments. Four of Sayer's ideas seem particularly pertinent. First, a major social change has been seen in the nature of the relationship between schools and their communities. This has developed over the last four decades, and has challenged the 'monastic' tradition that characterized secondary level education, in particular, over the previous centuries. Schools had seen themselves as separate from the community, taking pupils from their traditional backgrounds and exposing them to new ideas and vistas. It was not until the advent of comprehensivization that the idea was seriously challenged in the secondary sector. Schools became associated more closely with their community, and sought increasingly to involve parents and external professionals in the work of the institution. This has been seen at its fullest development in the community schools movement, pioneered in Cambridgeshire and Leicestershire in particular, and this idea is explored more fully in Chapter 11 by John Watts.

Second, the nature of the relationship between LEAs and schools has changed substantially. LEAs have traditionally been powerful and centralized, and have been accused in many quarters of actively interceding to retain this central control. Schools were artificially detached from many of their stakeholders by the intervention of the LEA as agents or brokers. This development of a dependency culture is only now being challenged by the introduction of LMS. Schools are now being given the opportunity to court and manage their own external relationships. The changes in these relationships are examined in more detail in Chapters 3 and 5 by Tony Cobb and George Campbell, respectively.

Third, the young people passing through the schools and colleges of the 1990s are from a different culture from that of two decades ago or more. They have been exposed since birth to a more complex and sophisticated culture, both in terms of social processes and in terms of the wealth of experiences they have received. For curriculum planners this raises questions about appropriate teaching and learning styles, many of which draw on outside resources, expertise and personnel.

Fourth, there has been a growing demand for education to be an integrated system. Schools and colleges traditionally saw themselves as self-sufficient 'island economies' with little necessity for cross-border links. The growth of 'pyramid' consultation groups combining schools and colleges in different sectors was a growing trend throughout the 1980s, but the introduction of the National Curriculum following the ERA (1988), with its emphasis on curriculum continuity from five to sixteen and its demand for processes of liaison and record transfer at phase changes, has made this an essential move.

Beyond Sayer's four external pressures, though, it is useful to consider two more that have played their part in raising awareness of the need for managed external relations. Of central importance has been the pressure towards accountability in the public services, and education has not been isolated from this. The belief that all external audiences need to be able to see the benefits and justification of public expenditure is widely held. The pressure to forge and manage these links to the benefit of all stakeholders is a strong one. Furthermore, there has been the growth of a 'client-centred' culture in education and the recognition that education providers must tailor their provision to the needs and wants of individual consumers. A second force, from within education itself, has been the recognition of the value of a child-centred approach in work in the classroom. The end result of both pressures has been the same in that they push schools and colleges to be aware of the needs of all their clients, to involve them in curriculum planning and institutional management, and to place management of these external relations high on the agenda for action. Schools must, of course, be wary of a critical problem in the client-centred approach. It is difficult, if not impossible, for the 'consumer' to judge quality prior to 'purchase', and it is tempting, therefore, to tailor provision to the stated needs of consumers. However, it is clear that education has absolute standards of quality that it must maintain if it is to preserve any vestige of status or dignity. This standard cannot be compromised, even if it necessitates failing to satisfy some consumer demands. Education, in conjunction with professionals in related academic, vocational and professional fields, must set these standards, and not leave it to the seekers of political gain or electoral popularity to impose their inexperienced judgements.

EXTERNAL RELATIONS MANAGEMENT – THE STATE OF THE ART

External relations management is increasingly important to the work of schools, but how far have schools taken up the challenge? Weindling and Earley (1987), in one of the first studies of the role of secondary headship that included a consideration of external relations issues, noted that the only aspect of ER that was a focus of concern was the promotion of the school's image. This was undertaken with the primary desire to attract more pupils, and extended to the introduction of such changes as better links with primary schools and improving links with parents through changes to the system of 'reports' and the introduction of newsletters. Such recognition was by no means universal among new headteachers, though, and seemed to be more characteristic of those working in urban environments. Williams suggests that the interest in external relations that the headteachers demonstrate 'are not rooted in perceptions that focus on genuine "client concern" . . . [but] appear to reflect a recent shift towards overt accountability and a reciprocal protection of the school's territory' (Williams 1989: 15).

Williams also suggests that headteachers have little understanding of the development of the sort of 'organic partnerships' that are needed with most external organizations. A common perception among senior managers in education is that external relations are all about 'competition' and not about 'coalition' and 'co-operation', when in reality the successful development of these relationships depends on the recognition of the place of each and the skill in creating a judicious mix of all three. Furthermore, it is possible that the management culture of many schools and colleges conflicts with the aim of enhancing external relations. The strong leader with the high public profile may be effective in public relations terms, but this focus on a single individual may mean that the external relations roles and activities of practitioners elsewhere in the management hierarchy are overlooked. Perhaps a reappraisal of leadership style is an essential prerequisite for the institution of effective external relations.

Even in the period since 1988 there appears to have been little practical coherent change. Piecemeal consideration of individual aspects of ER strategy takes place in all schools, but a small study of schools in the Bournemouth-Poole area by Pike (1991) shows the limited development of co-ordinated planning. Of twelve secondary schools surveyed, only three had a formal external relations or public relations policy, and eleven depended on the inclusion of 'public relations' within the job description of the headteacher or a deputy as the mode for dealing with such matters. Only three target audiences were identified (feeder middle schools, the community and industry/commerce), and no school used any form of market research to identify needs and customers. There appears, therefore, to be little attention as yet given to the need for proper planning of external relations, despite the growth of institutional or whole-school planning in other facets of management.

PLANNING AND MANAGING EXTERNAL RELATIONS

The process of planning in education environments is now an accepted part of the managerial task, with the clear aim to 'integrate the various aspects of planning in the interests of improved effectiveness' (Hargreaves *et al.* 1989: 4).

Although the time involved in the planning process may be substantial, there are a number of clearly identifiable benefits of development planning, which have been summarized by Hargreaves *et al.* (1989) as:

1 focusing attention on the aims of the school in terms of learning and achievement by pupils;
2 providing a co-ordinated approach to all aspects of planning;
3 integrating long-term aims with short-term goals for the institution;
4 relieving stress on teachers by allowing them to exercise control over change;
5 recognizing the role and achievement of all staff in promoting change;
6 improving the quality and value of staff development;
7 strengthening the partnership between staff and the governing body; and
8 easing the task of reporting on the work of the school.

Few specific models of ER planning exist and none, to date, relates specifically to ER in a school or college context. Keen and Greenall (1987) consider in detail the development of a PR programme within higher education. Devlin and Knight (1990) undertake a similar task within the school framework, as do Forster and Ives (1990). Gray (1989), and Cave and Demick (1990), consider the specific management challenges of marketing, albeit through a process which emphasizes the value of PR. The model proposed here is related specifically to the broader field of external relations, and contains a number of distinct stages in the planning process.

Stage 1: Undertaking an external relations audit

This is a prerequisite for the development of any plan, as it identifies the 'initial conditions and constraints'. It is, in essence, a top-to-bottom review of the institution from an external relations viewpoint, and may itself be divided into a number of sub-stages.

Stage 1A   This involves seeking the answers to a number of key questions.

1 Who are the internal and external audiences or stakeholders of the institution?
2 What external relations activities currently include or influence each of those stakeholders?
3 Who in the institution is undertaking those activities currently, and what staff time and other resources are being applied to those processes?
4 What expenditure and income are involved in those processes?
5 How and by whom are the existing overall external relations strategies being managed?
6 What resources – facilities, plant or staff-expertise – relevant to ER are not being used to the full?

Stage 1B   This involves making a comparative study of other institutions with similar educational objectives in a similar environment. In a commercial environment this exercise would be termed competitor analysis. This clearly poses problems of access to sensitive information, and any such study may be constrained by such problems. It is, nevertheless, essential to try to gain some feel for what other institutions are doing.

Stage 1C   This involves identifying the institution's external relations practice and needs by surveying the views of key external and internal audiences. This client analysis identifies the attitudes, responses and views of those groups that are partners in the institution's ER activities, and focuses on identifying what needs they have from the relationship with the institution. This relates to all stakeholders, but further analytical tools may be used to establish information relevant to the marketing of the institution. Researching the markets is clearly a complex and time-consuming process, and within financial constraints it is impossible to launch an extensive marketing research programme. Davies and Scribbins (1985) examine in detail the issues and processes of marketing research, and also identify the sort of 'market data' that may be available from the LEA, the school's own records and published government data. An additional approach is to undertake a 'buyer behaviour exercise'. This considers the factors that influence the decision-making of customers, and seeks to estabish which facets of a school or college need to be emphasized in the marketing process. It is easy to make assumptions about the importance of different factors on the basis of one's own perceptions. However, as these are the perceptions of the 'supplier', they may not reflect the real priority of the 'customer'. How important are factors such as school uniform, GCSE results, the nature of the school prospectus or the appearance of the reception area when parents or potential students arrive for their initial visit? Some ideas have been identified for higher education (Shattock and Walker 1977, Keen and Higgins 1990) and for secondary schools (Hanford 1990), but each institution needs to analyse the buyer behaviour of its own market.

Stage 1D   This considers the position of the institution within its operating environment. Two analytical tools are commonly used at this stage – environmental analysis and SWOT analysis. Environmental analysis involves a consideration of all aspects of the institution's environment to discover what processes and changes in that environment are occurring that may influence the school or college. This may include awareness of political, social, economic, technological, educational, legal, resource, demographic or environmental factors, all of which may impinge on the work and aims of the institution. SWOT analysis is an examination of strengths, weaknesses, opportunities and threats, and provides an indication of the potentially fruitful opportunities and directions for the institution, and the threats to be avoided. Devlin and Knight (1990) provide a detailed consideration of SWOT analysis.

Stage 1E   This considers the existing external relations goals as perceived by senior management, including the headteacher or principal, the senior management team and the governors.

Stage 1F   This involves the production of a report of the audit. This will obviously convey the factual findings of the audit process, but will focus on the identified problems and issues within the current external relations practice in the institution. Major areas of concern are likely to include: mismatches between the activities of the institution and other schools or colleges that appear to have a detrimental effect on the overall educational performance of the school; differences in perception between stated goals and actual achievements or processes, or between the stated goals of different component parts of the institution, or between internal perceptions of the nature and effectiveness of specific ER links and the views of the partners in those links; and previously unidentified ER impacts and consequences of the institution's educational or managerial processes.

Stage 2: Establishing external relations objectives

The audit process is intended to identify the key external relations issues. These are likely to relate either to specific fields, such as links with the LEA, links with industry, school–parent links, pupil or student recruitment, and aspects of institutional identity and image, or to improving the management and monitoring of external relations processes. The setting of objectives in these areas is the next task, and will require a consideration of time and resource constraints, and must be realistic and achievable. The precise nature of the objectives will be determined in large measure by the overall educational aims of the institution, and will reflect the 'mission statement' determined by the governing body and the headteacher.

Stage 3: Producing an external relations plan

The external relations plan is designed to facilitate the achievement of the objectives. It will contain specific tasks in relation to each objective which have clearly identified time scales for their operation and clear resource allocations for their achievement. Obtaining the resources may be a challenge to school managers. Keen and Greenall (1987) suggest that the funding can be derived in one of four ways:

1 allocate a fixed sum per student enrolled to be allocated to external relations activities;
2 see what other institutions spend and match it;
3 budget what can be afforded at the beginning of the financial year; and
4 allocate finance on the basis of the costed marketing plan.

It is clear that the fourth of these is the approach that is most likely to see the achievement of specific external relations objectives, but where resources are being transferred from other fields or denied to other activities the justification for such expenditure has to be clear. The challenge may also be made that spending public money on external relations activities is less than moral. For some ER activities it is easy to justify expenditure by recourse to simple cost-benefit analysis. For example, money spent on marketing can be demonstrated to be more than repaid by enhanced recruitment, and this may be deemed to be an increase in the efficiency of the use of the school's financial resources. A second area of activities is one where it is less easy to justify the expenditure of public money. This relates to spheres such as lobbying to influence political decision-makers, and funds for such activities may need to be raised from voluntary contributions or fund-raising events.

Stage 4: Implementing the plan

Implementation is essentially a monitoring process ensuring that each element of the programme is put into practice at the right time and in the right way. This will need some overall monitoring, which may fall to the SMT but may be more effective if undertaken by a separate External Relations Committee. Devlin and Knight (1990) suggest that such a committee may have members drawn from all sections of staff and management, perhaps chaired by a governor or a deputy headteacher. The value of such a group lies in its responsiveness to the needs of the whole staff, and the development of staff ownership of the plan.

Stage 5: Evaluation of the external relations plan

External relations management is a continuous process. The progression from audit to planning to implementation is not really linear but cyclical. The process that drives this continuous progression is evaluation. Successful evaluation is a planned, structured process that monitors the achievement of specified goals and targets *en route* to the achievement of objectives. It constantly reviews how the external influences and controls are changing, and reconsiders the plan's objectives. In most schools, as evidenced in many of the following chapters, the process is only *ad hoc* and reactive, however. There would seem to be a need for the evaluation process to be a key role of the External Relations Committee, which will need to monitor three aspects of the process: the management of the implementation phase; the quality of the products of the programme; and the effectiveness of the programme in achieving its stated aims and objectives.

CONCLUSION

Educational management is characterized by its diversity and demand (Torrington and Weightman 1989), and both these facets have become more prominent in recent years. The legislation of the 1980s has forced school and college managers to take on responsibilities across a much wider spectrum, with a particular demand for financial management skills and for an external focus to what has become an increasingly client-centred environment. The increased demand for active management, along with legislation, has also diversified the range of individuals involved in the managerial process. The headteacher in schools has changed role to that of chief executive, while the chair of governors and the governing body have become the equivalent of the company chairman and the board of directors in place of their advisory role of the past. It is becoming less common for senior managers to be personally and practically involved with classroom work, and the appointment of senior managers from outside education is now seriously considered in many institutions (Williams 1989). Furthermore, real accountability is being laid at the door of managers in schools, where the institution's recruitment, liquidity and long-term survival are now theirs to manage.

Perhaps the biggest challenge is the assumption of new roles.

In the immediate post-ERA period the centrality of financial management issues has perhaps overshadowed the management of external relations. However, the need for increased expertise in this field is clear. Ballinger (1986) identified it as an important focus of senior management staff development needs. Weindling and Earley (1987) demonstrated that, despite a perceived need for ER expertise, new headteachers felt remarkably ill equipped to take on the challenges. In the early 1990s, unpublished research undertaken by MA students at the University of Southampton demonstrated that among a small sample of headteachers and college principals in the Hampshire, West Sussex and Dorset region there was a clear lack of long-term planning in external relations management, and an equally clear vision among them that a small move towards some active marketing of courses and institutions was an adequate response to the challenges in the field.

This book aims to address a range of external relations issues from a practical management perspective. In the following chapters, authors with real practical expertise in their chosen field consider the issues and potential responses to them. It is hoped this will contribute to an expansion of the external relations horizons of governors, headteachers and other senior managers in schools and colleges.

Chapter 2

The organizational framework for external relations

Tony Bush

The Education Reform Act 1988 (ERA) has had a major impact on the management of external relations in schools. The Act's emphasis on competition has encouraged a radical reappraisal of the way in which schools relate to their various 'publics'. The external world is regarded increasingly as critically important in generating clients and securing the income that is dependent on successful recruitment. The changed climate of external relations is stressed by Sayer:

> The relationship of school and context was formerly a grey area, an extension of normal school organization, little considered and less esteemed in the practice of schooling. It is now quite clearly and starkly the priority for future development in both the practice and the theory of management.
>
> (Sayer 1989:3)

The low priority formerly accorded to external relations was reflected in the absence of a coherent structure for its management. While deputy headteachers, for example, might be responsible for curriculum management or staff development there was rarely a matching responsibility for external relations. Even in the immediate aftermath of the Act, Williams (1989) could assert that 'relatively few schools have policies or planned procedures for contact with their publics other than with governing bodies and parents' (Williams 1989: 18). Those external relations functions that were undertaken in the pre-ERA period were usually considered to be the responsibility of the headteacher. In their study of secondary headship, undertaken before the ERA, Weindling and Earley found that 'the head occupies a crucial position as mediator between the school and the wider community' (Weindling and Earley 1987:

164). This was even more evident for primary headteachers, who are closely identified with 'their' schools by members of the community (Coulson 1985).

The Education Reform Act has forced a radical reappraisal of schools' approaches to external relations, a process that is by no means complete. The next section examines the relationship between organizations and their environments, and points to the need for schools to be responsive to their communities. Subsequent sections feature different models of school organization and a discussion of two case studies of the management of external relations, one of a primary school and one in the secondary sector. The chapter concludes by suggesting ways of structuring the management of external relations in both primary and secondary schools.

ORGANIZATION AND ENVIRONMENT

The Education Reform Act has heightened the need for schools to be responsive to their external environments. The provision for more open enrolment means that schools cannot rely on a captive market denoted by catchment areas. Rather, they must compete for clients in a process redolent of the marketplace. Given the close relationship between recruitment levels and income, sensitivity to market needs may be a prerequisite for survival. In this sense schools are 'open systems', interacting with their environments and adapting to the changing requirements of their publics. Hoy and Miskel argue that schools must change their organizational frameworks, as well as their attitudes, if they are to thrive:

> Organizations such as school systems are now viewed as open systems, which must adapt to changing external conditions to be effective and, in the long term, survive. The open-system concept highlights the vulnerability and interdependence of organizations and their environments. In other words, environment is important because it affects the internal structures and processes of organizations; hence, one is forced to look both inside and outside the organization to explain organizational behaviour.
>
> (Hoy and Miskel 1989: 29)

Responsiveness, then, is a matter of survival. Sensitivity to market needs relates directly to the self-interest of the organization. The degree of responsiveness depends in part upon the permeability of the boundaries between the school and its environments. The greater the permeability, the greater the degree of responsiveness. The Education Reform Act has served to increase permeability by giving power to the consumers of education rather than to the producers. In this way it forces schools to respond to their environments rather than seeking refuge in isolation. 'The older tradition of bounded institutions set apart from their local communities will be replaced by the development of interdependent relationships' (Williams 1989: 23).

The permeability of school boundaries has also been increased by the enhanced role of governors. Their increased powers inevitably led to a reappraisal of the relationship between professionals and laity in the management of schools. Until recently, governing bodies were often perceived as external groups with a largely formal role. They now enjoy substantial powers and professional attitudes are still adapting to the new reality. 'The relationship between professionals and laity in education appears to be in a state of flux, and the potential for conflict between these two interests is clearly evident' (Pascal 1989: 89).

The governing body is at the heart of the post-ERA school rather than at the periphery as before. Because it represents many of the school's constituencies, it is well placed to act as the centrepiece of the school's external relations strategy. As we will see in the following sections, the organizational structure for external relations must include the governing body if it is to be a really effective framework.

MODELS OF ORGANIZATION IN SCHOOLS

If the management of external relations is to be successful it should be integrated into the wider organizational structure of the school. This is necessary partly to reinforce the centrality of external relations policy, but also so that the external dimensions of decision-making can be considered alongside the internal aspects. Williams asserts that external relations tasks 'should be the responsibility of everyone engaged in the internal organisation, management and functioning of the school' (Williams 1989: 20). In this way, the external implications of policy would be recognized at every level of management.

There are several different models of organizational structure in schools. These represent alternative normative statements about the most appropriate ways of managing schools. The five main approaches are the bureaucratic, collegial, political, subjective and ambiguity models (Bush 1986). The first three of these perspectives appear to be particularly relevant to the management of external relations.

All these models adopt different stances towards the management of external relations. They suggest alternative approaches for the organization of links with the environment. The normative assumptions about school organization provide a range of different models for schools to consider as they plan their external relations strategies. The main features of these models, and the patterns of external relations management suggested by the different theories, are as follows.

Bureaucratic models

1 Schools are represented as hierarchical structures emphasizing vertical relationships between staff.
2 Schools are typified as goal-seeking organizations with head-teachers taking the leading role in determining aims.
3 Managerial decisions are thought to be made through a rational process. All the options are considered and evaluated in terms of the school's goals. The most suitable alternative is then selected to enable those objectives to be attained.
4 Leadership is portrayed as a 'top–down' process. Headteachers possess authority over other staff because of their official position within the school. Orders flow down the hierarchy while information flows to the top.
5 There is a strong emphasis on the accountability of the school to its governing body and the LEA. Typically, the accountability centres on the headteacher who is held responsible for the successes and failures of the school, and is also the focus of communication with both bodies.

The emphasis given to accountability is the main determinant of external relations policy in schools typified as bureaucratic. Here the focus is on the school's need to be answerable to formal bodies such as the LEA or the governing body. Decisions are conditioned by internal judgements about the likely reaction of these formal groups to the proposals emanating from internal sources. Other external groups are de-emphasized except in so far as they are represented within the formal structure.

This stance has obvious implications for the school's organizational structure. Major decisions tend to be the preserve of those senior staff who interact most closely with the main external groups. Emerging policies are tested against perceptions of their likely acceptability to these formal bodies. Inevitably, headteachers and their deputies are those most likely to be able to judge these external desiderata. This reinforces the 'top–down' or vertical character of the organizational structure. It also suggests a requirement for the relationship between the governing body and the staff to be kept at a formal level, with the headteacher reporting to the governors rather than working closely with them.

Collegial models

1 Collegial models stress the authority of expertise in contrast to the positional authority associated with the bureaucratic models. Professional staff possess authority arising directly from their knowledge and skill. Professional authority arises when decisions are made on an individual basis rather than being standardized.

2 School staff are assumed to share common values inculcated during training and the early years of professional practice. These common values are thought to lead to shared institutional goals.

3 Collegial models assume that decisions are reached by a process of consensus. The common values are thought to provide a basis for reaching agreement about school policies. Any differences will be resolved by discussion rather than conflict. As headteachers do not have a monopoly of wisdom they cannot impose their views on professional colleagues.

4 Organizational structure is portrayed as lateral rather than vertical. This reflects the assumption that in professional organizations there should be the widest possible participation in decision-making.

Collegial models characterize decision-making as a participative process, with all staff having an equal opportunity to influence policy and action. Because expertise is thought to be widespread within the school, participative approaches are considered to be the most effective.

A major weakness of this perspective is the potential tension for headteachers who may be trapped between the desire to encourage participation and the need to be accountable for decisions arising from this collegial process. Headteachers are answerable for decisions which may not enjoy their personal support. This may serve to modify participation, in practice, as headteachers decline to endorse those recommendations that they feel unable to defend to external stakeholders.

In the post-ERA climate it may be possible to overcome this problem by incorporating governors in the participative framework. The governing body has the main responsibility for setting school policies, and it also enjoys representation from most of the main stakeholders concerned with the success of the school. If decision-making structures incorporate governors, the disjunction between participation and accountability should be greatly reduced. The potential is for a partnership between professionals and laity, working together for the benefit of the school and its pupils. This approach extends the notion of collegium to include lay governors as well as professional staff.

The concept of partnership will require a different approach from some well-established headteachers familiar with the traditional model of headship, where the professional leader is the effective decision-maker with the governing body having only limited and largely formal powers. Williams distinguishes 'on the bridge' headteachers from 'team leaders' and suggests that the former will face problems in adjusting to the new reality. 'The tradition of the "great person" as head of a school in an isolated, commanding position is demonstrably unreal and obsolete in the practice of managing schools' (William 1989: 26). As more than half of all headteachers believe that their school governing body has too much power, it appears that most have yet to embrace the partnership model.

Political models

1 Political models stress interests and interest groups. Individuals are thought to have a variety of interests that they pursue within the school. Staff with shared interests may come together to form interest groups. An example of an interest group in a secondary school is the academic department.
2 Political models emphasize the prevalence of conflict in organiz-

ations. In pursuing their interests, groups may come into conflict with other units in the school that have their own objectives.

3 In political models, decisions emerge after a complex process of bargaining and negotiation. Interests are promoted at committees and on more informal occasions. Resolution of differences may be protracted as groups seek to pursue their interests in several different settings.

4 Ultimately, conflict is likely to be resolved according to the differential power of the protagonists. Interest groups build coalitions in support of their objectives and the most powerful alliance is likely to succeed. The relative power of coalitions depends on their size and composition. Groups including several senior staff are most likely to prevail.

In political models, relations between schools and their environments are portrayed as unstable and ambiguous. Stress is placed on the different goals of various external groups. They may link with internal interest groups to press sectional claims, perhaps for more resources. The governing body may be one setting for such conflict.

Headteachers may be able to influence decision-making by engaging in political activity. Hoy and Miskel (1989) refer to the strategy of co-optation where leaders incorporate supportive elements in the environment into the school's policy structure. The provision for co-opted governors gives headteachers an opportunity to strengthen their position and enhance their prospects of favourable decisions.

ORGANIZING EXTERNAL RELATIONS IN SCHOOLS – TWO CASE STUDIES

There has been little empirical work on the organization of external relations in the post-ERA period. Inevitably, therefore, comments about the efficacy of particular modes of external relations management tend to be speculative. In a modest attempt to address this problem, I visited two schools, one primary and one secondary, to assess how their headteachers approached the task of managing their environments in the new climate.

Both schools are in the London commuter belt. The 11–18 comprehensive school has a five-form entry with a sixth form of 109. The school is recruiting in line with its standard number of

150 and the 1991 school roll was about 850. The junior and infant school has a one-form entry. It is oversubscribed but loses a few children to the private sector at the age of seven. Its 1991 roll was 200.

Interviews were conducted with both headteachers, and I also consulted relevant documents. While these discussions with busy practitioners yielded valuable data, the limitations of the approach are obvious. The perceptions of the headteachers are central but they were not 'triangulated' by observing meetings or by gathering data from other staff or governors. The discussion that follows should be regarded as indicative of developments at the two schools rather than as a definitive statement of their external relations policies.

The primary school

The primary headteacher points to the impact of the ERA on the school's links with external groups. As a result, 'external relations are now a very high priority'. She regards external relations as a 'whole-school responsibility', involving all staff, teaching and non-teaching. All teachers take charge of links with one or more external groups. The main responsibilities are as follows:

1 primary/secondary liaison;
2 nursery/primary liaison;
3 links with appropriate agencies in respect of special needs, health and welfare;
4 subject co-ordinators liaising with the relevant LEA advisors and with other schools;
5 liaison with the local community regarding visits, visitors and events; and
6 links with colleges of education in respect of teaching practices.

In addition, all teachers have a front-line responsibility for links with the parents of children in their class. This includes the organization of parental involvement in the classroom and consultation with parents, the fostering of an 'open door' policy and involvement with the school association.

External relations are managed through staff meetings. Most issues arise from staff discussions, are subsequently developed by the headteacher and her deputy, and are then brought to the staff meeting for consideration. One example is the issue of external

communications, where staff discussion has served to raise awareness of the importance of good communications with external
groups and individuals. The headteacher says that 'staff do make
suggestions, take and lead initiatives and have discussions, with
and without me, but do always ask my opinion and keep me
informed'. This comment implies that decisions are made on a
participative basis.

The governing body now has a major role in determining school
policy. The full body meets twice a term and there are also three
sub-committees, established at the headteacher's request. These
sub-groups deal with pupils, finance, and site and buildings. The
governors have invited the deputy headteacher to all meetings.
The children's sub-committee focused on special needs during the
spring term of 1991, including visits to classrooms to assess language problems. The headteacher says that this was done to enable
governors 'to have an informed discussion about aims, policies and
resources in respect of children with special needs'. The sub-
committees all have teacher representation, suggesting a partnership model between governors and professionals. Another example
of this approach is the involvement of the chair of governors in
staff meetings – for example, to discuss the 1991–92 budget.

The secondary school

External relations at the secondary school are managed by the
senior management team (SMT), which comprises seven staff: the
headteacher, two deputies, two senior teachers and two staff with
Department of Education allowances. Two of these staff have
major external functions. One is responsible for links with industry
while the other deals with services to parents, 'pupil culture' and
the school ethos. The headteacher 'provides the vision' and has
responsibility for links with governors.

The headteacher adopts a range of styles in leading the SMT
and the school. Initially he adopted a bureaucratic approach,
'planting himself as boss', to avoid bartering over issues he
regarded as non-negotiable. Subsequently there has been a change
to a more collegial style: 'we are aiming to share values'. He notes,
also, that the SMT may be the setting for conflict, adding that
this can be useful or 'cathartic'.

The governing body meets twice a term and there are also sub-
groups with specific functions, for example, to deal with finance.

The headteacher regards governors as 'partners', partly because of the influence of the ERA and partly because of the nature of the people concerned. The headteacher has invested considerable time and effort in attracting suitable parents to become governors because he sees them as likely to be very committed to the school. He was influential in persuading two officers of the parents' association to become governors and also encouraged the governing body to bring in parents as co-opted governors. This strategy is in line with the approach noted by Hoy and Miskel (1989), where leaders incorporate supportive elements into the school's policy structure to strengthen their position.

Governing body meetings are attended by the headteacher, both deputies and, where appropriate, the bursar. Training evenings have been held 'to build up a team feeling' and a joint governing body/senior management team training day was held to determine the school's aims. The headteacher says that 'this was a good day in terms of rapport'. These close links between the senior professionals and lay governors are in line with the partnership model discussed earlier and suggest that governors may be involved with the formulation of school policies rather than simply rubber-stamping decisions made by the SMT.

CONCLUSION – ORGANIZATIONAL STRUCTURE FOR EFFECTIVE EXTERNAL RELATIONS

The external environment and the governing body

The conceptualization of schools as 'open systems' implies that there is a close relationship between changes in the external environment and internal developments. Schools adapt in response to external stimuli so that they can survive in the new climate. Those that fail to recognize environmental change will be unable to respond to it. Schools that can anticipate change are most likely to respond effectively to environmental demands. In the external relations context, 'the most effective school structure is one that adjusts to the dimensions of its environment' (Hoy and Miskel 1989: 40).

However, schools have to consider internal considerations as well as external pressures in designing their structures and formulating their policies. School leaders and other teachers have their own views on how to manage the school, based on their professional expertise and their day-to-day experience of life in the school. External factors form only part of the data available to managers in determining how best to organize their school. Leaders have a responsibility to communicate their vision as well as to respond positively to the environment. 'The overall implication for practice is that school organizations do not have to be simple passive instruments of the external environment' (Hoy and Miskel 1989: 43).

In practice, there have been significant changes in organizational structure in many schools as a result of the ERA and the earlier legislation relating to governors. The newly constituted governing bodies have more authority and their composition enables them to represent many of the school's main external and internal constituencies. In view of these momentous changes, the governing body should now be regarded as a major conduit for the transmission of opinions and perceptions from the external environment. The participation of parents, teachers and community representatives, together with its legal responsibility for the school, makes the governing body the legitimate forum for reconciling external pressures and internal considerations.

Towards a partnership model

The incorporation of external interests in the formal structure may enable schools to develop a new mode of working based on partnership between professionals and laity. As we noted earlier, a major impediment to a more collegial approach to school management is the tension between participation and accountability. As long as headteachers were answerable to external groups for internal decisions, they could resist those collective policies that did not enjoy their personal support. Even where they were keen to advance the collegial ethic, the demands of accountability tended to limit the extent of participation in practice.

In the new climate, accountability is largely, if not only, to the governing body. As governors are more involved in the decision-making process, the tension between participation and accountability is greatly reduced. They will be working with teachers in determining policy instead of simply responding to proposals emanating from a separate, internal, decision-making process.

The evidence from our two case-study schools is that managers have been working much more closely with their governors since the ERA. At the primary school, the governing body's three sub-committees all have professional involvement. The secondary school headteacher has worked hard to develop a partnership with governors through joint senior management team/governing body training arrangements, as well as by the development of sub-committees with both professional and lay involvement. These developments have two clear benefits. First, governors are more aware of the implications of their decisions because of their involvement in policy formulation as well as decision-making. Second, teachers are more conscious of the external considerations influencing policy. The improved understanding on both sides can reduce tension and lead to a creative partnership for the benefit of pupils.

Another factor inhibiting collegiality may be differences in philosophy among the staff or between the professionals and the lay governors. Headteachers have tended to adopt a more participative approach when their aims are congruent with those of their colleagues. Headteachers are likely to appoint staff who share their educational values, and may then be able to encourage collegiality in the knowledge that decisions are more likely to be in tune with their shared philosophy (Bush 1988).

Similarly, headteachers may seek to influence the appointment of governors to ensure support for their own ideas. The headteacher of the case-study secondary school worked hard to encourage suitable parents to become governors because he thought they would be more committed to the school. We noted earlier that this process of co-optation offers headteachers a measure of control over the school's external environment. It also enables them to be more relaxed about governor participation in policy-making. An essentially political strategy is used to create a more favourable climate for collegiality. At its best, the outcome could be a partnership between lay and professional interests that both enhances the reputation of the school and caters effectively for the needs of its pupils.

Part 2

Links with the educational environment

Chapter 3

From paternalism to partnership: links with the LEAs

Tony Cobb

A feature of the early 1990s is that few people involved in aspects of managing the education service feel comfortable. There is a growing demand for in-service help with issues like planning and prioritizing, stress management, the use of time and resources, inter-personal skills and the rapidly changing industrial scene in relation to teacher salaries and contracts. It is arguable that head-teachers have gained in confidence during the last two years. The practice of delegated funding has produced results better than the worst fears, and the career development and salary needs of senior managers are being more widely recognized.

Counterbalancing this trend, colleagues within local education authorities (LEAs) appear to be twitching visibly and too often about their futures. This is hardly surprising. In August 1991, Howard Davies, Controller of the Audit Commission, wrote: 'I see as a government view that authorities are, for the most part, an encumbrance to the reform agenda rather than a means of achieving it'. (Davies 1991). He argues that the education environment has changed significantly since the Audit Commission (1989a) counselled against the view that 'LEAs are entirely redundant, since they no longer directly control educational institutions'.

This chapter will contribute some aspects of thinking in relation to the need for a support network, like a reformed LEA or different tier of organization. How far can schools survive largely on their own, using marketing consultancies and whatever centralized organization is set up by government to fund and evaluate their work? Inevitably, my background in secondary schools, including sixteen years of headship in two comprehensives, will colour these observations. They will also be influenced by the rapidly growing cries from headteachers for professional support and information on ways of managing change within our schools. Some change is seen as helpful; some as conflicting in its effects; some as downright unhelpful. A common feature of coping strategies is the need to find contacts and consultancy that share recent good practice in many of the newer areas of management faced by schools.

It is, however, hardly surprising that LEAs should be feeling twitchy about their futures. For so long they have been the major institutional source of support for schools, but present political comment and action give little encouragement for their future survival. Clearly, the principle of open enrolment, the marketing of schools and delegated budgets based on pupil numbers will be developed and strengthened in the 1990s. Whatever the electoral fortunes of the major parties, there is very little evidence to suggest that the present moves to grant-maintained school (GMS) and city technology college (CTC) status by schools and colleges will be reversed. In practice, it would be a very unpopular move for an articulate section of the population – apart from the logistical implications. Present soundings suggest that a further 2,000 schools will move towards GMS status now that the electoral colour for post-1992 is clearer. The removal of 16–19 provision from LEA control is also significant. The present government review of Her Majesty's Inspectorate, and the constant pressure on LEAs to delegate more of their funding directly to the schools, calls into question the future role of any external organization in relation to the school's responsibility for managing its own affairs. In county and borough halls, there is an inevitable feeling of instability, justifying Howard Davies's view that LEAs are beginning to lose good staff because, as organizations, they 'seem to have drifted into that category of unloved and unwanted institutions for which no easy alternative can be found' (Davies 1991).

Does there need to be an LEA or an alternative? In introducing the Citizens' Charter, John Major has emphasized the increased influence of parents in the running of schools, which has echoes in Labour Party policy. Michael Fallon talks of the 'residual functions of the LEA, the social service functions of attendance and special needs, advisory functions and of quality control' (Fallon 1991). He is particularly concerned that the LEA providers are also the evaluators in the quality control debate. Given the flavour of these introductory comments, it is the view of some influential voices that the future of the education service can be put largely into the hands of discerning parents, allowing market forces to reward the successful and provide the resources, which lack of pupil numbers will deny to allegedly ineffective or unsuccessful schools. The same voices support the need for a reformed inspectorial service, to include observers from outside the professional field. There is a growing underlying feeling that the best barometer for indicating present and future success will be the numerical strength of the pupil roll, measuring local confidence and satisfaction very quickly. Published league tables of measurable results will help the undecided to form a judgement.

Is even our level of democracy quite ready for this, admittedly caricatured, scenario? We are into local management of schools, for better or worse. This 'marriage' of management between professionals and the local community will need to be serviced by some kind of organization able to call upon readily available evidence of good practice, of research, of methods of evaluation – of the national educational scene. A headteacher and a school governor need the same support as a magistrate receives from his qualified clerk; that a hospital administrator receives from his professional consultant; that an industrialist receives from his own professional bodies. Many governors do recognize their own amateurism; many headteachers recognize their own loneliness. Neither will question their own accountability; they just want an accessible form of supportive help.

IN SEARCH OF QUALITY

'A major responsibility of Local Education Authorities is the quality of education' (Audit Commission 1989b: 3). The use of the word 'quality' is now as familiar a piece of educational jargon in mission statements and school aims as the idea of 'the caring school'. Quality control, quality assurance, performance indicators, success criteria; how quickly these expressions have become part of the language of school managers. The School Management Task Force, writing of the character of effective schools, suggests: 'The concern for excellence in business organisations has been paralleled by the search for excellence in schools' (School Management Task Force 1990: 5). Essex LEA, for example, has adopted the phrase 'quality through partnership'. The word 'quality' is in!

Perry (1991) looks at the meanings of phrases like 'quality assurance' and 'quality control' in relation to the work of the LEA inspector/advisory services of the future. Her important theme is that any effective form of future evaluation of schools must rely on encouraging the professionals within the service, and the managers of the service to take ownership of the quality issues. This thought needs to be developed alongside the view of Sams, who muses, 'just think what we could achieve with a real partnership and trust on both sides' (Sams 1991).

Interviewing applicants for teaching posts was one of the most demanding parts of my job as a headteacher. Arrogant enough to believe that I knew what I wanted, I then found it quite difficult to answer one or two of the questions I had prepared for candidates. What had I expected them to say? Was I just wanting to know that they had thought about the question at all? Some specifics were expected when candidates were asked to define the essential characteristics to be observed in good classroom teaching. Alternatively, what qualities should be evident in a well-educated sixteen-year-old, about to leave school? In many cases a feature of the interview was the struggle of the candidate to answer that question confidently and with some clarity. Take the back of an envelope and attempt one of them for yourself! In applications for headship, one LEA asked for a 200-word definition of a rounded education. Requests of this kind are difficult for all of us because we assume a common understanding among all colleagues of the purposes of our daily teaching. An attempt at definition becomes as all-embracing and cliché-ridden as the average set of school aims – and I have composed a few of those. What is 'the quality', that we seek in our education service – and where do we look for a standard or an evaluation of our own efforts?

Open enrolment, market forces and league tables place a strong emphasis on achievement that can be recorded. Recent political statements are beginning to confirm earlier suspicions that the National Curriculum standard assessment tasks (SATs) would revert to paper and pencil tests fairly rapidly. Once testing had been established in the major areas of experience – English, maths, science and technology – there would be sufficient evidence to begin evaluating and comparing the results of schools across the country.

For some, it is the results that are all-important, rather than the methods or content of what and how children learn. These results will indicate the quality and effectiveness of the school. That simplistic view needs to be examined against evidence from those schools bold enough to ask for parental views from the catchment area. A school in Dudley LEA has done this for two years, and the statistical evidence of examination results is not the parents' first or even early priority in measuring their satisfaction with their school. A respected deputy headteacher, with whom I once worked, commented that many parents are much more concerned about whom their child sits next to than the final measured results achieved – which is not to deny their importance. Advocates of quality assessed by testing and results need to look at what a parent seeks when he or she talks of the happiness of their child.

A second, simplistic evaluation of quality within a school can relate to its cost-effectiveness. The unit cost per pupil may become as important a statistic as the proportion of sixteen-year-olds achieving GCSE grades A–C. The point will not be laboured here because some faith is placed in many parents who are aware of the present funding levels, evident in the maintenance of school buildings, provision of equipment and accessibility to curriculum extension activities. Parent–teacher associations have a long history of 'making good' and for some time HM Inspectorate has been interested in collecting details of supplementary funding of this kind. Parents will not easily equate quality of education with cost-effectiveness, although political encouragement is being given to those who are willing to 'top up' existing formula funding. Governors and headteachers will need some source of neutral guidance about curriculum entitlement for pupils and the support funding it requires. They must avoid the understandable but deceptive delight achieved by good housekeeping. For example, £15,000 saved in one year can give an extra young member of staff, a number of computers or yards of carpeting, but only if an objective eye is kept on the answer to the question, 'Was there a cost in the quality of education experience offered to our pupils last year?'.

Both these examples – quality assessed by results or by cost-effectiveness – underline the need for each school to look at its own understanding of the meaning of quality within the education service. While both areas have a contribution to make to the discussion, school managers are going to have to develop a school vision that goes beyond either immediate political expectations or management by hunch based on the experience of be-taught-as-I-was-taught. The obvious danger in delegated local management is insularity of views and objectives. Competitiveness and marketing will also distort the clarity and appropriateness of some of the aims and activities seen as priorities for teacher energies. However sophisticated our democracy may appear to be, those offering to manage our schools may not always come from a background as experienced and successful managers in other fields and may be hard pressed themselves in difficult economic times. Handy's (1989) analysis of the shamrock organization of many working groups underlines that those with creative or managerial ability are already working much harder in their chosen occupations.

Whatever the faults of the present structure, Sams (1991) is right to emphasize the advantages of the accumulated experience present within the LEAs that might provide the constants and the comparative evidence needed by those charged with managing schools. There is a goodwill and working knowledge among individuals within LEAs that is too valuable a resource to be lost by mishandling present changes in the management of schools. It should not be left to the entrepreneurial skills of a handful of this number to exploit the present and future situations by setting up consultancies, which may or may not reflect the balance of support agencies needed by schools to make sensible decisions and to manage organizations successfully.

Safeguarding the quality of education experienced by pupils is important, but not easy. Listen to a group of seasoned inspectors discussing classroom observation and agonizing over how pupils learn – and how that process is to be observed, recorded and evaluated. That is a professional skill. It is also a generally neglected one. For some time now, school senior staff have been preoccupied with the pace of management changes that have not focused on classroom teaching. Mel West, addressing 350 teachers within the Coastal Confederation of North Essex in July 1991, made the point that there is a sharp divide in language and understanding about basic National Curriculum concerns between groups of classroom teachers and the senior managers of schools. For too long the priorities and objectives of these groups have been very different. Crudely assessing the pupils has become a separate activity from the running of the school.

A number of us see appraisal – better still, staff review and development – as having the positive advantage of putting the quality of classroom teaching at the top of everyone's agenda. Once that debate starts, governors, headteachers and senior staff are going to need the advice and experience of those who are inevitably much more practised in this field – and they are to be found in the ranks of advisors, inspectors and advisory teachers.

There is a problem of credibility for some, particularly those who have been out of schools during the last decade, but there are many astute practitioners whose observational skills many headteachers would be wise to study. Together we can make progress towards quality in the pupil's learning experience.

SERVICING SCHOOLS

Most headteachers seek out contact with each other. The LEA has provided a framework, through meetings and courses, of opportunities for collective and informal discussions. Meetings of professional associations are seen in the same light, and some of the best management development for headteachers comes from these contacts. The chance to nobble a colleague, to test a personal view, to ask for clarification on a new initiative; all these anxious inquiries give meetings a value that may take priority over a sometimes unappealing agenda. Coming together is what is important. Many headteachers and deputies have been likened to the proverbial swan: composed and serene on the surface, but paddling desperately to keep going within a tide of changing practice. The policies of open enrolment and marketing are going to make those open, positive exchanges of information much more difficult, at a time when access to information and shared good practice is sought so desperately.

The School Management Task Force has recognized the need to promote structured forms of cross-fertilization. As a result of its report (1989), and its important emphasis on school-based management development, the task force has set up a pattern of regional consortia, based on the LEA structure, looking at effective means of and areas for supporting governors, headteachers and senior staff in the management of schools. Four principal areas have been identified:

1 the use by schools of training materials for management development;
2 the need for support networks of information for headteachers, governors and senior staff;
3 the development of personal profiles or portfolios and accreditation opportunities for teachers; and
4 the identification and provision of efficient management services for schools.

LEEDS METROPOLITAN
UNIVERSITY
LIBRARY

With limited funding, LEAs have been encouraged to pursue action research projects, co-ordinated nationally and led by 'independent' bodies, usually based in management development units or higher education. The first investigations were completed in March 1991 and work is now developing on agreed projects, generally within the four areas outlined above.

In a very short time, and in embryonic form, a network has developed to provide schools across the country with current information. The areas identified for development arose out of the first year's investigations, and were requested by staff in schools. Good practice is being shared within and across LEAs. It is arguable that the task force, and the more neutral role of regional co-ordinators, has acted as the necessary catalyst to get development work activated. The limited funding of £60,000 over two years for each consortium would not have been a sufficient attraction in itself. There is a willingness to work together. Basically, I believe that LEAs were interested in taking part for the same reasons as headteachers wish to get together periodically. Some LEAs are well ahead in their own thinking in part of the four areas identified for projects, but, large or small, ahead or still at the starting blocks, LEAs were anxious to know what was going on elsewhere and to compare that with their own individual progress.

In the marketing future, how far will this kind of collaboration be possible? The present exercise has had to meet and overcome problems of working together – ownership, jealousies, competitiveness – but the scale of the problems increases if more schools become independent of any local co-ordinating influence. Valued initiatives of this kind are also expensive in time and money, and it is doubtful whether individual schools could see this kind of research and development work as high on their priority list, although they would admit to wanting the results that accrue from the work done. It may be that groups of headteachers, or their local associations, will provide a future developmental grouping, but experience suggests that this is dependent upon the qualities and leadership of individuals and the chemistry of relationships. Before any terminal decision is taken on LEAs, some thought has to be given to the arena for co-ordinated development and action research, and the means of circulating good practice. The government's wish for rapid change needs an accompanying feeling of confidence and reassurance among its work-force. That is best gained by making it quite possible for one school to see its advances mirrored in or mirroring the good practice of others.

A number of LEAs have seen the value of establishing a service philosophy and are actively promoting practical service support. There are obvious areas:

1 technical advice – for example, law, finance, site management, industrial relations, personnel management, information technology, appeals;
2 management development – for example, available training materials, off-site training opportunities, development in personal profiling and accreditation, succession training, salary policy, appraisal;
3 school development planning, business plans – for example, strategic planning, prioritizing, monitoring and evaluation methodology; and
4 consultancy advice – professional dialogue: 'I need to talk to someone who is not in school.'

It is assumed that most LEAs provide some level of service in each of these areas, while some are well ahead with planned support for schools under a number of headings. The difficulty for them is that each heading represents a potential call for help from any school, and the newness of national policies does not allow experts or experienced professionals to respond readily. Schools need advice, but many senior colleagues and governors need to feel confident that practical help is being given by those who have previously shared experience of the particular problem.

Survival for LEAs, and a service welcomed in most schools, may depend in the future on the growing practice of using serving heads as specialists or consultants in specific areas of support. A small team working together, particularly in the newer initiatives of the Education Reform Act, could provide a source of commonsense approaches to changes demanded in schools. A team drawn from several authorities would be less threatening, better informed and likely to encourage a wider use of good practice where it is found and developed. The previous suggestions of an inward-looking conceit within some LEAs should not be repeated many more times within schools, all determined to do their own thing. Education is about searching out and sharing our knowledge and skills. The education bandwagon of the 1990s will move more awkwardly if it is supported by individually re-invented wheels, wasteful of so much personal energy and effort.

The Audit Commission has recognized a value in the co-ordinating role as part of the support service for schools. It defines six different approaches for LEAs as part of a successful future strategy. It argues that an LEA should be:

i) A leader, articulating a vision of what the education service is trying to achieve;
ii) A partner, supporting schools and colleges and helping them to fulfil this vision;
iii) A planner of facilities for the future;
iv) A provider of information to the education market, helping people to make informed choices;
v) A regulator of quality in schools and colleges;
vi) A banker, channelling the funds which enable local institutions to deliver.

(Audit Commission 1989a: 2)

Comments by many headteachers, senior staff and governors suggest that services of this kind would be welcomed. However, the credibility and usefulness attached to that proffered range of services would depend upon other factors.

1   Increased evidence of genuine partnership between all sectors of the service. Teams that provide the leaders, partners, planners, providers, regulators and even the bankers of the future need to draw equally upon all the skills and experiences available to them. If LEAs continue, they need to strengthen the growing practice of mixing officers, administrators, researchers, evaluators and those presently in our schools, where the latter can offer so much immediate experience of implementing rapid change and innovation. Authorities vary, but previously this last group has tended to be informed rather than genuinely consulted at the earliest stages of policy-making. Given the direct delegation of management to schools, it is very much in the interests of LEAs to encourage a working partnership that not only aims at sensible solutions to current problems, but establishes a confidence in and reassurance about the separate abilities of the contributors. Sadly, I feel that it is too late to consider the fixed-term 'job swaps' between officers, advisors and headteachers that would have gone a long way to improve the professional thrust of the service, at a

time when politicians seem to be ascendant in outlining future aims.

2   A greater and more evident willingness by LEAs to seek out each other's strengths, acknowledging that even the largest authority cannot fully provide every service needed by schools. The marketing climate militates against this, but it also wastes service energies and duplicates activities. Schools have an entitlement, just as their pupils have. They are entitled to receive, through informed networking, information about important successful initiatives beyond the LEA boundaries. In articulating a vision of what the education service is trying to achieve, the leader role of the LEAs would reassure schools and increase confidence if they acknowledged that their policy statements were drawn from the perceived strengths of the service wherever it operates. That is particularly important for the parts of the service that an individual LEA feels are in specific need of urgent development. Understandably, so often, schools need practical help today rather than the promise of a policy tomorrow.

CONCLUSION

Teachers are creative people. Governors will include creative thinkers. Both groups have experience in planning and problem solving. What need is there for any additional 'service'? The Audit Commission comments:

> Some schools and colleges may find it easy to establish governing bodies with the motivation and competence to manage with very little support from the centre. Elsewhere this will not be true in the short term, and perhaps not in the long term either.
>
> (Audit Commission 1989a:4)

Stillman and Grant (1989), commenting only on the work of advisors in LEAs, give a number of personal comments supplied by headteachers, including those drawn from the most negative, 'or perhaps just more honest'. Having recognized the need for more management training for advisers and inspectors, there is also the recognition that headteachers can be slow in seeking advice themselves. One is quoted as saying, 'We have a certain inbuilt arrogance that might prevent this.' There are also comments that confirm the constant complaints about the lack of availability of hard-pressed LEA staff.

Few disagree with the realistic view that delegated local management has given more creative power to headteachers, senior staff and governors. Consultation and accountability have increased, but headteachers, particularly, have the chance to create a vision of the future of their schools, resulting from local decision-making and future control of the allocation of resources. It is not a facile comment to suggest that a traditional deference to the role and judgement of the headteacher continues, as all those who consult with a headteacher have some distant memory of their own school-days. Those who have held the post will see the advantages of these several factors combining, but will also recognize that an already 'lonely' position can become even more isolated by virtue of its increased power. How often have headteachers been grateful to observe some earlier decision of school policy-making, which has not worked successfully, and to blame the part, real or imagined, played by the LEA in the formulation of that policy? Equally, some headteachers have found good allies using LEA officers in the handling of contentious issues with governors. Many headteachers have confessed to reactive management planning in the 1980s, forced upon them by the speed and range of changes required by national policy. How many headteachers are natural readers of professional writing? How many have time to research the objective evidence necessary to contribute to lasting decisions? The evidence of my present job, offering management development support in the West Midlands, is that many headteachers would welcome a continued formalized structure for support, professionally based and offering quality advice on the best available methodologies and practice. They also need the certainty of an available arena for shared reflection, consultation and problem solving.

The opportunity for LEAs is clear. This chapter has avoided one of the more contentious debates. In some form an inspectorial role will continue, and the government is addressing the future form of that at present. Can an LEA successfully handle that issue, if it is to continue to be part of its role, and still offer support services and consultancy to headteachers, who will want to share their thinking frankly and openly to make progress? I still believe that the credibility of inspectors, whether individual appraisors or inspectors of schools, depends upon a simultaneous willingness to offer support as part of the total process. Others believe that the two functions are mutually exclusive. As one HMI commented to me, 'you need to see a school through the (independent) eyes of a child'. The child's one experience of school cannot admit excuses in the delivery of the service. The debate continues.

It is on the continued provision of efficient support services that this chapter has concentrated. The term 'inspector', and even 'officer', has unfortunate historical associations barring easy acceptance in the new climate. For those holding senior posts in the LEA or in school, the terminology is still suggestive of a hierarchical relationship, rather than the servicing, supportive role that could become the way of the future. Legitimate or not, the possible causes of tension, created perhaps by mutual feelings of suspicion and sometimes insecurity, need to be removed for both parties if a feeling of genuine partnership and teamwork is to emerge.

It is evident that LEAs are also looking at their staffing costs and restructuring is resulting, with its consequent losses, particularly among advisory teachers. There is more evidence of fixed-term contracts and performance-related pay. If LEAs are to survive as a valid servicing agency for schools, a decision that secures their future will have to be taken so that the service attracts good staff with career development possibilities. The present hiatus is not good for anyone and, at worst, could leave schools with the further problem of having to distinguish between the varied qualities of different, independent consultancies, springing up in the vacuum created. Some salary levels presently offered are also going to leave a difficult credibility problem to be faced by those appointed in their dealings with developing differentials within schools.

If LEAs were to disappear tomorrow, would there be pressure for their reintroduction in some form in the foreseeable future, as some believe? Would schools combine to create a support service on a cost-sharing basis? Would national government be forced to create a DFE-led larger bureaucracy, which the Prime Minister is supposed to fear? I believe that the majority of headteachers, staff and governors, when reflecting upon and planning school development, recognize the need for an informed, co-ordinated and efficient support agency.

LEA or not, it is clear that such a future agency or agencies would depend for their future upon funding by schools for the services given. That fact would go some way to ensure quality of delivery. It is the genuine, positive professional need for the right kind of help and information that should form the basis for better partnership in the future between provider, client and support service. It stands more chance of long-term survival than politically imposed reorganization of any kind. Even now, collectively, within the education service, we could make a partnership work, which would provide real advantages and a more successful future for all our children. The result would be greater job satisfaction for all.

Chapter 4

Links across the primary/secondary interface
A primary perspective

John Messer

> The National Curriculum will offer a broad and balanced education for all pupils providing progression and continuity from 5–16 and beyond.
>
> (National Curriculum Council 1990a: 3)

THE GREAT DIVIDE

Over many years, there have been innumerable local initiatives designed to create bridges between the primary and secondary phases of education. Sometimes the initiative has been born of some simple social motive linked to easing pupils' physical transition from one phase to the next. More recently, there have been genuine attempts to secure some progression and continuity of learning. Often the creation of some form of transitional progress report has formed the tenuous basis of a link. The attempts have been well meaning and have received varying degrees of support, yet very little real progress has been made towards creating proper durable structures between what has now become Key Stage 2 and Key Stage 3 of the National Curriculum.

The causes of such failure are often identified in superficial terms. The physical distance between establishments is a common explanation. Alternatively, the idea is presented that, although all educational establishments are sailing in the same race and heading in the same general direction, individual schools have a tendency to present themselves as distinctive autonomous units that defy any attempt to subsume them into a general and common educational movement. The real causes, however, are more to do with ethos, culture, philosophy and differing perceptions of good educational practice.

BRIDGING THE GAP

Primary schools have very few problems with continuity of practice between Key Stage 1 and Key Stage 2, even where separate infant and junior schools have been established. A common notion of good primary practice, which is generally supported by HM Inspectorate and developed by a well-informed LEA advisory service, pervades the primary phase. This notion is also well supported by the National Curriculum programmes of study and National Curriculum Council guidance.

> The full potential of the ten subjects will only be realised if in curriculum planning schools seek to identify the considerable overlaps which inevitably exist both in content and skills. Inter-departmental planning can lead to more coherent development of skills and the reduction of wasted time and over-loading caused by duplication of effort. In due course, it is likely that schools will throw all attainment targets in a heap on the floor and reassemble them in a way which provides for them the very basis of a whole curriculum.
>
> (National Curriculum Council 1990a: 1)

The cross-curricular approach advocated by the National Curriculum Council is already practised by many primary schools and is perceived as the cornerstone of good primary practice. While continuity of practice is not a problem between Key Stage 1 and 2, there have always been question marks hovering over the issue of progression throughout the primary phase. Practitioners are often not confident that the topic or project approach precludes overlap and sometimes development is impeded by permitting patches of negligible progression. Usually this occurs because planning systems are deliberately not totally systematic and stiflingly prescriptive in order to leave room for spontaneity. Generally, though, a common philosophy translates into a common perception of sound educational practice in the primary phase.

Established primary practice does not survive the transition from Key Stage 2 to Key Stage 3. There is a primary/secondary curriculum divide that yawns wide and stretches deep. Practice considered normal on one side of the chasm finds no recognition on the other. While broad educational philosophies may be shared, the structures developed to satisfy such philosophies have grown from a different historical basis. The National Curriculum insists that there will be a continuum from age five to age sixteen. Rhetoric, however insistent, will not create such a continuum.

It is for LEAs and school managers to determine how best the gulf can genuinely be filled and a smooth continuous path created. Certainly, the need is recognized as demanding urgent attention, but the task is daunting. Should secondary schools begin to adopt more primary practices, particularly in the area of cross-curricular thematic approaches? Will the compartmentalized National Curriculum destroy the topic approach? Will primary schools be forced to abandon their perceptions of good practice in order to cram the required curriculum content into their crowded day? Perhaps curriculum planning could itself cross the divide. Perhaps learning policies could be jointly constructed by pulling together primary and secondary planners. The first step along this path is pointed out by the National Curriculum Council:

> The successful management of the whole curriculum depends upon a corporate plan for the whole school, embracing all the aspects of the whole curriculum as augmented by each school in the light of its individual circumstances.
>
> (National Curriculum Council 1990a:7)

The emphasis on individual schools ploughing lonely furrows, albeit in the same direction, is not necessarily a broad enough vision of corporate planning. A better model could be based on the creation of wider consortia stretching across the phases.

CORPORATE PLANNING

Admittedly the National Curriculum has pushed primary schools further towards whole-school corporate planning and away from individual teachers planning in isolation. This is often corporate to the extent of including Key Stage 1 and Key Stage 2, even if in different establishments, in a co-ordinated process. The prescribed programmes of study have forced primary schools to create a clear, yet integrated, topic framework that may include cyclical project planning, often on at least a two-year basis to avoid any overlap that could be occasioned by vertical grouping. While there is undoubtedly resentment that such planning could destroy the facility to capitalize on some unexpected occurrence, most teachers accept that a framework is inevitable, but plead that the plans must not fit so tightly as to stifle chances to follow children's natural spontaneity.

POLEMIC INTO PRACTICE

One of the major managerial tasks imposed by the National Curriculum is, then, to translate the hope of progression and continuity into practice. It is an issue with such deep organizational implications and with such wide-ranging financial consequences that few have yet been able to make the required mental leap.

Most primary schools have accepted the more immediate demands of the Education Reform Act and have developed plans for the integration of the statutory programmes of study into their normal teaching routines. As they become more familiar with assessment procedures it is abundantly evident that the old *ad hoc* transfer report, usually compiled to assist transition between phases, is, however comprehensive and however carefully structured, simply not good enough. Soon primary schools will be reporting that, in any one subject, pupils will be functioning at any level up to 6 and even beyond. All these achievements will have been generated from a mixed ability and possibly 'mixed age' group.

Any one child is likely to be functioning at differing levels in each of the nine National Curriculum areas of learning. The interface profile at transition might be plotted, as in Figure 4.1.

It may well be difficult to tease out any homogeneous patterns. Confidence in the validity of the assessment and its reporting will strengthen over time because the teacher assessments (TAs) will have been confirmed by the standard assessment tasks (SATs) at the end of Key Stage 2. The results will have been reported to parents. Governors will know of their responsibility as summarized in the opening paragraph of *School Governors – the School Curriculum*:

> The purpose of the school is to educate all its pupils to the maximum of their potential. This means offering a curriculum which is right for every pupil.
>
> (DES 1991a: 1)

It will be increasingly obvious, however, that every pupil has very different educational needs. Schools with a deeply rooted tradition of organizing children into rigid age bands taught in class groups will find it difficult to create programmes of study tailored to the

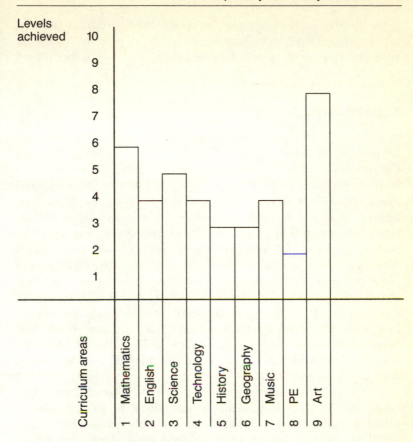

Figure 4.1 An individual's transitional 'interface profile'. Many different combinations are probable

individual and designed to create progression with no time-wasting curriculum overlap. However carefully setting or banding by ability has been organized, the precise and detailed range of information cumulatively emanating from the assessment procedures, coupled with heightened parental awareness and expectations, will create severe pressures requiring radical re-evaluation of organizational structures. Secondary schools may consider breaking year group moulds to allow the extension of vertical grouping, often practised with year 5 and year 6, to year 7 and year 8 in an effort to produce the flexibility required to offer a wider range of study levels. A logical extension would be to break down subject and departmental barriers in order to create cross-curricular patterns of learning. School managers would have to plot the course of such dramatic changes with infinite precision and with due regard to all implications.

FEDERATION

It is generally accepted that curriculum delivery frameworks will be planned in order to create vehicles for rationalizing National Curriculum programmes of study into a coherent whole-school learning programme. Such a framework will ensure that all attainment targets are covered and that unnecessary duplication is avoided. Cumulative teacher assessment will eventually be formulated over a period of years rather than during a frantic period in March each year. All such planning initiatives could be converted into more than a whole-school corporate initiative. There is a perceived need for planning that involves a cluster or federation of catchment area feeder primary schools as well as their secondary counterparts. It is ridiculous that many neighbouring schools are independently beavering away without reference one to another. Many differently shaped wheels are being invented with no attempt to consider cross-phase liaison directed and briefed to achieve coherence.

Cross-curricular impetus generated by the National Curriculum could dissolve some of the compartmentalized subject approaches in the secondary sector, especially and initially across years 7 and 8. Close planning liaison with the federation of primary school planners could well create a continuity of approach and avenues of progression through years 5–8.

Some LEAs are endeavouring to lend support to local initiatives and some are finding central funding to promote the formation of federations. In Wiltshire, the foundations for such initiatives are long established but their objectives rarely go beyond easing transition from one phase to another. They usually take the form of implanting well-equipped primary school classrooms on the site of the parent secondary school. This classroom is used for transitional visits by year 6 children so that they can feel there is a secure base within the secondary campus from which to venture into the secondary playground, lavatories and refectory. This is particularly effective in easing the transition of primary pupils from small rural schools. In such cases, year 4, 5 and 6 children may all visit for a week or more to gain a continuity of familiarity. The primary classroom is also programmed for use by year 7 secondary pupils. It affords opportunities for secondary teachers to observe primary colleagues working on site, while also giving secondary teachers the opportunity to practice primary organizational techniques with their year 7 or 8 pupils. It can only work well where headteachers and faculty heads are prepared to allow teaching groups to opt out of the secondary timetable for a complete and extended period of time.

Bradford-on-Avon, in Wiltshire, is served by a highly regarded 11–18 comprehensive school that draws most of its pupils from two large urban primary schools and four small satellite village schools. The secondary headteacher is very keen to promote primary–secondary liaison, not just for reasons of policy but also to create common practice. He envisages a 10–12-year-old common curriculum that bridges the phase divide. This could stretch from years 5–8. This common transitional curriculum would be supported by common classroom practices.

The LEA is supporting this project by providing twenty supply days designed to allow secondary colleagues to work alongside primary colleagues, as well as to allow primary teachers to work in the secondary phase. The LEA funding is much more than matched from the catchment schools' delegated INSET budgets. The objectives are more than merely acquiring an appreciation of the different models of teaching: the prime purpose is to explore pathways designed to promote common curriculum planning, common methods of delivery – a continuous problem of learning experience for individual children – and a commonality of purpose in relation to shared goals and educational objectives. Much is expected from a small input of funding, but these essential ingredients have propelled the plan into action:

1 goodwill and a desire to break down the barriers that create isolated units of education both within a school and between schools;

2 a perception that the great divide might be counter-productive; and

3 a mutual respect and growing realization that primary and secondary teachers do not necessarily embrace opposing educational philosophies but, rather, many share educational beliefs.

It is, however, as difficult for secondary colleagues to erode subject barriers as it is for primary colleagues to accept the possibility that the National Curriculum, and the desire to give every individual child entitlement to the utmost of his or her potential, may necessitate greater specialization and specific teacher expertise in the primary phase. Each phase seeks to embrace any transplantable good practice identified in its cross-phase relationships.

The first step for the secondary phase is to allow far greater inter-faculty flexibility. The primary phase must accept that children working in the higher levels of attainment, perhaps levels 6 and 7 in the core subjects, might need access to teaching modes not traditionally associated with primary schools.

CENTRIFUGAL PRESSURES

Like many satellite primary schools and the secondary schools they feed, the schools in Bradford-on-Avon meet increasing pressure to form closer links. The National Curriculum, with its requirement to create a curricular continuum, may be the strongest impetus, but there are other equally persuasive reasons for clustering closer.

A large slice of 'special needs' funding has been devolved on an area basis. This creates the requirement for headteachers and perhaps school special needs co-ordinators to examine the special needs of the children within the area. They are empowered to use area funding, according to criteria that they themselves devise, in an equitable and effective way, to satisfy the special needs of pupils within their area. In practice, the funding is so limited that it usually means no more than agreeing to use the money to employ an area special needs support teacher, usually with 'remedial reading' expertise, and determining how the hours should be divided between the schools. A more radical, although less integrated, approach could be to place the teacher in one school for a longer period with a brief to create intensive short-term programmes of study designed to satisfy the special needs of groups of children collected from the federated schools.

Instrumental music tuition and peripatetic music teaching are being delegated in many areas to individual schools. The schools are often choosing to use this delegated money on an area basis by putting their share back into a consortium purse, from which to purchase an area music teacher. I could not afford a whole specialist music teacher for my school, but I can benefit from a part of such a teacher, not only purchased by the federation but also directed to create a coherent area music policy, provide area-based INSET, draw together and utilize latent musical expertise or equipment that might be lying dormant in the area schools and integrate music not only in a cross-curricular way but also across the phases.

Competition between schools has, paradoxically, also given impetus to a federated approach to marketing. The Bradford-on-Avon primaries are so confident that they share a common purpose, a common curriculum and common practice that they are planning common marketing strategies and a common prospectus of the facilities offered by the Bradford-on-Avon group of schools. The LEA has conducted 'general school evaluations' of these schools and the consequent, well-informed LEA overview has resulted in the recommendation that the various strengths and specializations found in the neighbouring schools could be better shared. This pulls schools closer together and persuades them that the conflict that could be generated by fierce competition and aggressive marketing are not in the best interests of the area's developing educational service. Few headteachers really believe that it is in the best interests of children to uproot them from their residential milieu and transport them to a distant school that follows the same curriculum as the normal catchment school.

Secondary schools seem to be more seriously affected by competition and some seek to use primary school platforms to promote their own particular brand of education. We have available many school prospectuses from LEA and private schools, both in the immediate vicinity and further afield. We have such confidence in the local comprehensive school and such a vested interest in its continued success – largely because it is at the centre of our area's initiatives – that it is unusual for us to recommend any other school. Other schools may be considered if they offer any special facility – academic, sporting, artistic or remedial – that would match any individual's needs and that was not sufficiently developed in the local school.

State schools also have a vested interest in retaining LEA finance within the LEA for local needs. If a single child escapes to an independent school then, according to the dictates of LMS, the school loses funding for that child. One primary child represents funding in excess of £1,000, so any loss of pupils is significant. If the child remains in a state school within the area, the area continues to benefit. If the child is seduced by a state school across the border into another LEA, not only does the parent school lose, but so does the LEA, which has to pay its neighbour for the cost of that child's education. Again, then, competition tends to make a group of schools close ranks against competition from the independent sector, schools in other areas and, more particularly, schools in other LEAs.

All these pressures whirl around the area and pull our schools closer towards a confederated, protectionist, educational stance. It is doubtful whether this was foreseen as a consequence of the Education Reform Act.

WHOLE-CURRICULUM MANAGEMENT – SOME PRACTICAL STRATEGIES

The National Curriculum is created by the formation of a number of curriculum building blocks, but the model is constructed in several dimensions. One is over a period of time – the whole of compulsory schooling – broken into time zones described as Key Stages. The curriculum design cuts right across existing phase boundaries. Another dimension is that of coverage or the whole content offered to any one learning group at any one point in the timespan. When time and coverage are linked by process – the teaching and learning experiences offered – the whole-school curriculum is created. Federation allows whole-school curriculum policies to be developed. As well as being broad and balanced, such a curriculum must be coherent. Coherence is achieved by devising systems and practical strategies designed to ensure that individual pupils actually travel along paths that give them complete access to their entitlement.

If it is seen as productive to weld the phases together into some coherent form, ten areas for development could be considered. Many have been tried and tested in isolation, but real vision is required to implement a co-ordinated package involving all ten.

1   Occasional joint governors' meetings organized with the specific aim of identifying areas where a common approach could be beneficial and agreeing strategies to achieve some common policies. The governors, being the local educational policy-makers, should develop a heightened awareness of their responsibilities towards the wider community. It might be that they could devise common

stances and common policies that would serve the best interests of the town, the city or their area of a community. They could certainly gain from joining forces to solve common problems, not only *vis-à-vis* the LEA. If area funding is devolved, for INSET perhaps, they should certainly be party to decisions involving the allocation of such monies within the local area.

2   Identifying planning co-ordinators from each phase and creating a detailed brief of what they are expected to achieve by a certain date. We have found that co-ordinators appointed from area primary and the parent secondary school are notoriously good at talking about their own particular problems, but sometimes less good at sticking to a planning schedule in which clear objectives are set and tagged with a time restraint.

3   Establishing realistic allocations of time to allow co-ordinators to meet. This has serious budgetary implications, so commitment to any schemes must be absolute. All too often schemes are planned by a school's senior management team without sufficient regard to building in adequate time allocations. Time is an expensive and limited resource. Time is, however, often the enabling factor that translates plans into practice.

4   Observation of practice and teacher exchange across school phases as well as between catchment feeder schools. To gain a cohesive, unified approach to the 5–16 curriculum, the area schools must achieve a heightened awareness of the dynamics of the constituent establishments. One prerequisite is an open-door policy that allows teachers to communicate freely without having to refer to any element within a managerial or faculty hierarchy. Another is commitment, coupled with some mechanism that will prod teachers into actually leaving the confines of their own home establishments. All too often the pressure of work is used as an excuse to cancel visiting arrangements.

5   Joint cross-phase projects, usually of short duration but intensive in operation. Drama days can provide the vehicle for excellent area projects, with either all primary schools participating or preferably all schools, primary and secondary. Such days are usually the culmination of project work completed in the area schools. We

have, for example, participated in an Elizabethan Day using the Longleat estate as a focal meeting place.

6   School-generated proposals for LEA support. Some LEAs require persuasion to promote initiatives. If schools can prove a sufficient degree of commitment to any given project, great impetus can be generated by a successful bid to the LEA which may, in turn, be able to use the bid to gain funding from some satellite or central source.

7   Shared resourcing and facilities – to include human resources. Any audit of resources contained within area schools would reveal considerable duplication. Some duplication is inevitable, if only for reasons of convenience, but some resources could easily be shared if someone, somewhere, had responsibility for creating an overall register of the area's resources together with an evaluation of future requirements, perhaps fed on to a central computer.

8   Parental involvement where practical and the establishment of communication channels to keep parents informed. Parents can be prime movers in assisting the creation of an area identity for schools. If they can be encouraged to see the benefits that can accrue from schools working more closely together, the whole process gathers greater momentum. Individual schools generally send regular newsletters to parents. A termly area newsletter from all federated schools can help to create a mutually beneficial corporate identity.

9   INSET designed on an area basis. In-service training often happens on an uncoordinated ad hoc basis with a consequent dilution of potential effectiveness. This is particularly the case where schools have delegated, albeit earmarked, INSET funding which they use in splendid isolation without reference to the area schools. Greater efficiency and more effective targeting of INSET funding occurs where an inter-school, cross-phase approach can be organized.

10   Collaboration to produce recording and reporting systems which share some degree of commonality. Many individual schools are creating their own methods of recording each individual's

child's National Curriculum progress as well as school specific forms of report to parents. Many schools are developing effective systems; others are floundering in the face of the complexity of the task. Often there is limited central direction or advice. Where areas pool ideas and develop an area system of recording and reporting, schools benefit from mutual support whilst any pupils transferring schools within the area share a common form of documentation. The secondary school benefits from receiving a single transfer format rather than ones designed exclusively for individual feeder schools.

Areas require a co-ordinated approach and consequently a co-ordinator to develop any combination of these initiatives. Co-ordinators must cultivate mutual trust and respect. Any designated co-ordinators must share a common vision, coupled with the necessary qualities of leadership to translate plans into practice. Co-ordinators can be LEA funded appointees – such as advisory teachers or advisory headteachers. The post might be exclusively that of area co-ordinator or may be part of a larger role. The post may be part time, full time or job shared. Co-ordinators could be seconded from area schools to work according to a job description tagged with the appropriate incentive allowance. However the co-ordinator is created, their role is crucial to area curriculum continuity.

AGE WEIGHTED PUPIL UNITS – THE POOR RELATIONS

School funding is dependent not only upon the number of children it can attract but also upon the age of the pupils. The funding disparities between different age groups persists even where a common curriculum is being followed. In some areas a Year 7 pupil is worth twice as much as a Year 6 pupil yet the younger scholar may well be working at a more advanced level. The argument that primary school pupils require less in terms of books and equipment is no longer true, while equipping a reception class is at least as expensive as meeting the requirements of many sixth-form groups. The argument that a better pupil–teacher ratio is required in secondary schools has been discredited by the counter-claim that relatively mature secondary school scholars are much more capable of working in less intimately supervised groups than the five-year-olds in the reception year.

Generally, the primary sector throughout the nation believes that it is the poor relation and that no cognizance has been taken of the all-party House of Commons Select Committee Report (1986), which concluded:

> There is still, unfortunately, a tendency to regard primary teaching as 'second best', and to look upon primary education as a prelude to real education, and the differential resourcing of primary and secondary, to the disadvantage of the former, is but one aspect of this entrenched and misguided tradition.
>
> (House of Commons Select Committee 1986: 2)

The historical disparity persists, despite DES circular 7/88 which stated quite clearly that the LEA formula for funding schools 'should be based on an assessment of schools' objective needs, rather than on historic patterns of expenditure, in order to ensure that resources are allocated equitably' (DES 1988b: 1). The continuing funding disparity causes a tension between primary and secondary schools. While recognizing that any shift of funding from the secondary to the primary phase would cause justifiable resentment and long-term damage to inter-phase relationships, something must be done to secure a more equitable level of funding, at least for children in the transition years. There are problems. The secondary sector itself feels starved of resources. The budget is finite. A minimum requirement is that years 5–8 receive equal units of finance. Ideally, this should be achieved without damage to secondary phase funding.

A harmonious solution will not be easy, but some authorities have addressed the issue more seriously than others. The complete phasing out of age-weighted pupil units (AWPUs) in favour of pupil units, pure and simple, implies one of the following: a considerable shift of funding from secondary to primary; massive new investment in the primary phase; or the direction of resources released from the dismantling of central LEA systems towards the primary phase.

An individual's access to the National Curriculum entitlements could well be denied if grossly inadequate levels of funding continue. Planning procedures cannot reach fruition unless the facilitating resources are made available. It is in the best interests of the secondary phase to support a radical adjustment of AWPU so that firm foundations can be laid.

CONCLUSION

Primary schools have an obligation to think beyond Key Stage 2, while secondary schools should be planning from Key Stage 2. Together they should be collaborating to create a developmental curriculum designed to ensure that each individual has genuine access to a broad and balanced National Curriculum that promotes progress, fosters continuity and embraces a coherent set of systems designed to make it work. A curriculum that is perceived as effective and that meets the needs of individual children will inspire parental and public confidence. As a matter of urgency, all primary and all secondary schools must consider to what extent they are achieving the continuity and progression demanded of them by the National Curriculum. Budgetary and resource implications must be seriously addressed. Joint federated management plans within the broader LEA curriculum policy may be worth pursuing.

Schools can no longer function as autonomous, isolated units. We must all be prepared to sacrifice some degree of autonomy while embracing co-operative strategies designed to assist the individual child in gaining complete access to his entitlement.

Chapter 5

Links with educational support services

George Campbell

This chapter is concerned with the management of the links between a school and its educational support services. At the time of writing the local management of schools (LMS) is still in its early years, and how it will develop further is far from clear. LEAs are at different stages in the devolution of financial responsibility to their schools. Schools are displaying different levels of confidence and competence in tackling the many changes brought about by the Education Reform Act. Teachers are feeling under severe pressure in facing up to many diverse demands, at a time when their schools seem under-resourced and their own professional efforts and performance appear to be under-appreciated. The necessary infrastructures that could promote and foster improved communication and decision-making among school staff and their associates at this time of profound change are still being worked out and tried out. Against this complex and dynamic background, schools are being challenged to re-think the ways they might gain access to various educational support services, and to consider at a more fundamental level the cost and necessity of such provision.

What are educational support services? In short, they are the services, from whatever source, intended to facilitate the school's educational function, whether it be through the more effective learning of its pupils or the professional development of its teachers. In parallel with developments in schools, these services are themselves also undergoing profound change.

EDUCATIONAL SUPPORT SERVICES – THE CHANGING PERSPECTIVE

Before studying current developments, it is helpful to look back a generation to examine what the school's external links with its support services were in order to appreciate how much the scene has changed. A generation ago, the main external links were with Her Majesty's Inspectors, who provided a national overview of the schools, and with LEA officers and advisors who reflected more local and sectional interests. HMIs observed closely and kept up a running commentary on the quality of education being received by the children.

Among the early forms of external support emanating from the DES, and strongly promoted by HMIs, were the DES regional in-service courses jointly planned by HMIs, LEAs, higher education institutions and teachers to promote curriculum and staff development. The coming together of teachers from different schools with LEA advisors, HMIs and university and college tutors created many productive working partnerships, under discussion group conditions. These, in the longer term, promoted closer working links all round, and accelerated changes and encouraged new developments in schools.

The appointment of an increasing number of LEA advisors also dates from this period. While their function was primarily to have a critical overview of the teaching of a particular subject in the schools, they were often regarded by teachers as sources of power, particularly financial, and of influence over decisions concerning teacher promotion. They are also remembered for their evangelical zeal in furthering new methods of teaching and learning.

At that time, few advisors were appointed with inter-disciplinary duties. However, teams operated within a LEA, organizing day or short residential courses for their teachers primarily concerned with updating knowledge and methods, and giving some opportunity for hands-on experience of new equipment. Since then the teams have expanded, mainly into inter-disciplinary areas such as the humanities, health, personal and social education, and technology.

The careers officers located within the local authority organizations performed a useful task of locating vacancies for the many young school-leavers and assisting the latter in making wise choices. Frequently working in partnership with careers teachers, they did invaluable preparatory work in the schools, enabling the children to make an early transition into adult working life. This service has continued to develop, especially in the area of work experience.

Youth officers also occupied a role within the LEA organization. Although officially outside the school system, unofficially the more enterprising and imaginative cultivated the schools, in part to secure access to facilities out of school hours. The best worked closely with teachers to extend the range of extra-curricular activities both on and off campus. They also co-operated closely with careers colleagues in organizing exciting and novel residential courses for school-leavers. Increasingly, these courses became associated with the Duke of Edinburgh Award Scheme, offering expeditions and projects, and opening up new interests, and new and challenging environments, to the older children. Over the years activities of this type, valued for their contribution to the personal and social development of pupils as well as their enjoyment, have become important features of the school's extra-curricular programme.

Much of what has been outlined here could be described as developmental in assisting teachers and their pupils to reach new horizons. One other professional group which occupied a central position was primarily concerned with maintenance: the education welfare officers (EWOs). Their task was to liaise closely with the school over the children's attendance record, identifying any emerging patterns of unusual behaviour in school or absence. Any departure from the norm would be pursued with the parents and a report made to the school. The EWO became a co-ordinating reference point for reports from other services that might be involved, such as social workers, the family doctor, educational psychologists and the police, and hence held a central or pivotal role. The EWO remains a key member of the school's support system, working as a link person between the pastoral staff and a child's home.

Closely allied to the welfare of the child, although not a part of the LEA, were the school health and dental services. The school medical officers and the school nurses regularly conducted routine inspections of the children. So much effort was wasted in the classroom, then as now, in trying to get children to learn when their minds and bodies were preoccupied with the more basic concerns of hunger, cold, illness, neglect, abuse, poor sight or poor hearing. School health and dental services still work in schools, although now more proactively, helping to promote sound health and dental practices and to prevent ill health as part of broader health education programmes.

The home is agreed by most working in education to be the most important external source of educational support for the child. A generation ago, while there was adequate research experience to confirm this, the means of harnessing it was hardly developed, certainly not on a large scale. Parents' evenings were the major point of contact, their purpose ranging from open evenings to allow the community to view the school at work to individual discussion with teachers on a child's progress. Closer involvement of parents in school policy and decision-making was much less common, although the parent–teacher associations (PTAs), providing an early forum for debate and fund-raising, were gaining ground. Some schools and teachers were undoubtedly reluctant to share their position with a potentially strong power group; and some parents felt that teaching was the teachers' business and that they were best left to get on with it.

Over the years, parents have become more deeply involved in the education of their children, by the extension of PTA activities and, more recently, by recruitment to the governing bodies of schools. They now play a part in influencing curricular policy in such controversial areas as religious education and sex education.

The 1990s present a different environment for schools. Gone are the heady, affluent days of the 1960s and 1970s when requests for equipment and materials would be met instantly, classes were reasonable in size, and teachers had time and enthusiasm for extra-curricular activities and were strongly supported by a burgeoning advisory service. Careers officers, youth officers and EWOs were then much in evidence, working alongside the school and supporting its efforts, assisted by an increasingly well-informed parent body. Today, the scene is very different. Schools convey a sense of being beleaguered and under threat. Why is this? What has changed?

First, schools are generally under-resourced. Buildings are not maintained, repaired or repainted. Equipment, materials, books and stationery are not provided as generously as before. These are all a reflection of the tighter controls on national and local government spending. Budgets still appear to be large, but they purchase less.

Second, the expectations placed upon schools have increased despite the relative decrease in resourcing. The focus of the pressure is the Education Reform Act (ERA) as each of its many sections is implemented. There has not been the time to accommodate, assimilate and consolidate the numerous curriculum changes required and, as a result, overworked teachers have had to make do with hasty improvization before being forced to move on to the next innovation. In addition, there has been a heavy investment of time and energy in such developments as working with governors, planning curricula for sex and religious education, and introducing the National Curriculum.

THE ROLE OF INTERNAL MANAGEMENT STYLE

The need for support services has become even greater in the light of these changes, yet the delegation of managerial responsibility to schools means they must ensure appropriate provision themselves. Such services will not automatically be available and some will become more limited in supply than in the past. For example, as LEA advisors take on a more inspectorial role, so the provision of advisory services may need to be 'bought' in from elsewhere by a school. To ensure efficient and effective service provisions, schools must first of all examine their own management structures and methods.

Schools must devise effective internal lines of two-way communication and unified policies that are soundly based and clearly thought through before external links can be properly developed. Associated management styles should be sensitive to pupil and teacher needs and priorities, and therefore open, flexible and adaptable. This is to ensure that all sources of expertise are tapped through adequate consultation, and that planning and decision-making bodies are fully representative. In any innovation the sense of ownership of the enterprise has to be widely shared if high levels of commitment are sought. If not, it will be viewed cynically by those excluded and the chances of its successful implementation jeopardized. This is clearly a plea for the inclusion of those who most frequently feel themselves distanced from the plans of their school's senior management teams, in particular, the more inexperienced and junior staff, especially women.

To examine the links with educational support services and their potential for development, it is useful to view them in relation to school management styles. Broadly, it is possible to identify four basic patterns.

The 'top–down' style   This emphasizes individual achievement encouraged by a competitive spirit. There is strong central management control operating through layers of seniority which, while promoting an apparently efficiently run system with clear lines of communication and responsibility, may be in danger of being insensitive to well-informed views 'in the more outlying parts' or lower down the school. Delegation is limited. The organizational structure is clear cut, but with little flexibility; adaptation to change and innovation is limited. However, while this top–down approach dominates, it may not permeate to all parts. Thus, it would be possible in practice for a 'rebel' subject department to be run on more open and flexible lines, if the head of that department and colleagues were primarily concerned with working together as a team and building a greater self-awareness and self-confidence in their pupils, purely paying lip service to the central management system.

The 'top–down listening' style   This closely resembles the first, but with the important distinction of being sensitive to feedback from the peripheral parts. Thus, two-way communication is better developed. Central management will sometimes act on advice but not to any fundamental extent, especially where this might lead to a major shift in school policy and practice. Where policy is questioned, central management will aim to persuade and ultimately convince the questioner of the wisdom of preserving the *status quo*. As in style one, sub-divisions of the school, such as subject departments or tutor groups, may create counter cultures in which staff and pupils assume stronger roles.

The 'bottom–up listening' style   This recognizes and respects all groups, considers their observations and advice carefully, and attempts to incorporate them into school policy. A policy of devolution, properly monitored and managed, is the start. The existence of active working groups on cross-curricular themes or in relation to specific external links is an example. Programmes are planned, discussed and debated, and the results fed up the line, with senior management not only listening to but acting on the advice. Pupils in tutor groups, debating school or community issues, are listened to. They might have something original and important to say, and if they think they are being taken seriously they are much more likely to be serious. Accurate profiling and records of achievement rest on such a principle. Earlier initiatives such as active tutorial work (ATW) started the process.

The 'community action' style   This involves a much greater devolution of responsibility for debating and deciding major policy to all groups, including children. As all in the school community have a say, corporate responsibility and ownership are assumed, both for any school policy and for its implementation. One of the features of this style is a school council, which consists of pupils and staff drawn from all levels. Its purpose is to represent the views of the wider school community on matters of school policy and practice. A successful council debates a wide variety of school issues and earns the respect and trust of the wider school community by the wisdom of its decisions. One only has to visit a school where, for example, the physical environment has been 'improved' by the pupils planting shrubs, decorating walls and generally exhibiting a sense of responsible ownership of 'their school' to realize that, in practice, it works.

Obviously, there are examples of all four styles operating in most schools, but the question is, which style dominates? If it is not the 'community action' style, how accurate will the reading of the school's priority needs be, how unified will any sense of purpose be, how enlightened and realistic will any policy planning be and how successfully will the school identify the need for and secure the effective support of outside bodies? What is all too apparent is that unless the school management style is conducive to the promotion of a positive and constructive relationship with an outside body the latter will not wish to be involved, or, if it does, may operate only on a limited front. This could jeopardize the chances of the school attaining its key targets, for example, in the National Curriculum cross-curricular themes where the need for external reference points and the support of outside bodies are essential.

SUPPORTING NATIONAL CURRICULUM IMPLEMENTATION – A PERSPECTIVE ON SUPPORT SERVICE MANAGEMENT

It is appropriate to consider an example that is, in most schools, a priority case for the support of external educational services in the 1990s – the challenge of implementing curriculum change, and in particular the demands of the National Curriculum. Closely associated with the inception of the National Curriculum is the priority need of staff training and development. Hitherto, the LEA would have played the key role in any forward planning and ultimately in the in-service education and training of staff. However, the role of the LEA is changing, and while at the time of writing it is difficult to foresee what this might be ultimately, a number of scenarios can usefully be defined and explained that demonstrate the variety of ways schools may obtain support for curriculum development.

Under local management of schools (LMS), the LEAs were to have retained important monitoring, advisory and supportive roles. If staff development and training are to be high priorities, several alternative models of association of a school with its LEA in terms of educational support present themselves. The differences between these scenarios are based on the relative strength of the assumed LEA role in relation to that of the school. Further variations due to the arrival of private sector entrepreneurs will be studied later. The challenge for the school is to clarify which of these scenarios relates to its own situation.

LEA support scenario 1   Here the LEA maintains a strong consultative and advisory structure through its advisory officers and short-term seconded teacher-advisors. This team relates to the school at curriculum co-ordinator level as well as through heads of department or at other appropriate points, for example, cross-curricular themes. If done well the work is comprehensive and thorough. It is, however, time-consuming and expensive, and, in addition, can only be a stage in the school's staff development until the school takes over a greater share of responsibility. Ultimately, only an in-house programme designed by the school staff themselves will be entirely responsive to their professional needs.

LEA support scenario 2   This has school–LEA links that are far less strong and consist of a small LEA core team whose function is to monitor, consult and advise, as before. While their function and status are similar to those in scenario 1, their influence is considerably less, being fewer in number and meeting up with school staff less often. Obviously, such a service can only concern itself with high priorities on selective occasions, such as working through a strategic plan of in-service training for key staff. While close and regular contact will be maintained with the curriculum or in-service co-ordinator, the major responsibility for development will rest with the school.

LEA support scenario 3   This has at its base a strong school role with a LEA advisory officer in attendance on a regular basis, not unlike the education welfare officer. The advisory officer's role is to provide expert advice when requested by school curriculum planning teams.

LEA support scenario 4   This is the form that all schools will ultimately adopt. It assumes the school is an independent institution, directing its own policies, but in consultation with the LEA through its advisory officers. Such contact will be on a much less frequent basis than formerly and only concerning important matters upon which the school needs its advice, following an inspection, for example.

A further refinement of scenario 4 could be a voluntary grouping of schools, assisted by the LEA, similar to the TVEI school clusters, for example. The purpose would be to compare notes, share wisdom and problems, and identify and share resources. Within the cluster or group each school would be quite independently pursuing its own policies. On the other hand, the need for schools to maintain or increase the number of pupils on the roll in order to survive, along with the ending of catchment areas, leads to schools actively 'trawling' for pupils, often in competition with each other. If this competition increases, schools, far from being willing to work in partnership, will guard their special features jealously and so become more inward-looking and isolated.

FINANCIAL ISSUES IN SUPPORT SERVICE PROVISION

Throughout the examination of the school-support services relationship, no mention has been made of funding and finance, and of their management. The delegation of increased powers and responsibility to school governors and a corresponding diminution of the part played by LEAs has, at its core, money. Schools are now expected not only to plan for development in the years ahead but to pay for it, out of funds now being allocated to them. This entails deciding policies, setting objectives and planning programmes of innovation, for example, in staff re-training and development, which will have to be paid for out of their budgets. Clearly, in an organization as complex as a school, there may be many developments that require funding, so priorities will have to be decided and financial provision made for when the bills have to be paid.

The problem is that in addition to being complex organizations schools are also new to this situation of being financial managers and are being obliged to learn as they go; no easy matter when they are entrusted with the expenditure of a sum of money far in excess of anything any one member of staff or governor (except for a big business representative) has ever had pass through their hands. Early signs indicate that the schools are exercising great caution and some may even emerge in the first year of LMS as underspenders.

Deciding priorities for expenditure or investment in schools is a major headache. Getting the balance right is a constant struggle between materials and equipment, on the one hand, and staff training on the other. Often, the long-term investment has to be sacrificed to short-term expedience, especially where the funds are limited. If this continues, however, the cumulative effect of a shortfall in in-service education on the development of the teaching profession could seriously undermine the work of even the best schools.

School size is an important factor. Obviously, the larger schools are more secure financially in the competitive business of maintaining pupil numbers. They have more to offer with wider choices and their 'economies' are less likely to be affected by a slight fall in the number on roll. The smaller school, on the other hand, can find realistic forward planning very difficult when faced with even a small drop in pupil numbers, such as on the departure of a few families from the school catchment. Resources may then be stretched to the point where staff may have to leave.

EDUCATIONAL SUPPORT SERVICES – A FUTURE PERSPECTIVE

While an attempt has been made to foresee future developments in the management of key education support services, recent government legislation and policy statements may cause these to be further revised. What is clear is that all schools will be managing 100 per cent of their budgets and having to purchase services formerly provided free by the LEA. Will they purchase them? From whom will they purchase: the LEA or independent entrepreneurs? Let us study possible trends in three of them: the inspectorate, advisory services and INSET, and pupil welfare.

With regard to school inspectors, far-reaching changes have been proposed for both HMIs and LEA inspectors, which will greatly affect the nature, extent and quality of support that schools have traditionally expected to receive from both. The 'parents' charter' legislation will change the role of HMIs from inspectors of schools and advisors to government on education policy and practice, to a much smaller regulatory body of administrators who oversee the work of other school inspectors and do not advise governments. The 'other' school inspectors will be either from the LEA or some independent private organization. They will also be more strictly engaged in inspecting, primarily data gathering to determine the extent to which school performance and standards meet targets identified in the school development plan. It is proposed that these inspections will occur regularly at four-yearly intervals.

At first sight, inspectors are hardly candidates for a school support service. Yet as Eric Bolton, Senior Chief of HM Inspectorate has pointed out, had the new style of inspectorate been operating in recent years, 'HMI reports about the implementation of GCSE, teacher appraisal, the national curriculum and the introduction of standard assessments would not have appeared' (Bolton 1991). In this respect, schools looking to HM Inspectorate for national guidelines at a time when they are being increasingly pressed to do so may in future find the service wanting.

At local level LEA advisors have already been translated into inspectors and are having to master quickly new skills in keeping with their new roles and tasks. The assumption is that a regular four-year inspection by such local teams, whether LEA or private sector, will help improve the performance of schools. However, as Margaret Maden, chief education officer of Warwickshire, emphasizes, 'Such inspections represent only one aspect of current inspectorate activity. Last year [1990] Warwickshire inspectors chalked up more than 3,000 visits to schools, an average of ten visits for each school, and an actual minimum of six' (Maden 1991). This work largely concentrated on National Curriculum, LMS and teacher appraisal, ensuring that the schools met government requirements. The danger of relying too heavily upon the four-year inspection is that the frequent monitoring of the finer detail of school development in times of rapid change will be missed. This continual review and appraisal policy with support is currently what the best LEAs offer. Can it continue under the proposed new system?

An alternative two-tiered inspectorate with advisory team support is recommended by Eric Bolton (1991). It would consist of HM Inspectorate (about two-thirds of the present number) inspecting nationally, and regional inspectorates carrying out frequent inspections of schools. The routine inspection would be overseen by HM Inspectorate much as is envisaged in the parents' charter. The two bodies could be formally connected.

> For example, in national priorities for inspection, such as concern about the teaching of reading, there would be a specific national survey inspection by HM Inspectorate, and it would also feature as one of the issues to be addressed in every school inspection within a given period.
>
> (Bolton 1991)

The latter would be supplemented by more frequent advice and help from a reconstituted LEA advisory team or their private sector counterparts.

Associated with the newly emerging LEA inspectorates are new advisory teams consisting mainly of teacher advisors on short-term contracts. While their function is to continue to work with schools, advising and helping in those areas being inspected by their colleagues, their roles are becoming complex and difficult to manage.

One reason for this is LMS. With the transfer of all finance to the school, the responsibility for INSET goes with it. Thus, LEAs now have a very thin resource base from which to spearhead priority INSET unless it has government backing and funding. The net result of this is that advisory teams are having to apply complicated criteria to prioritize support, with the attendant conflict of roles that this process generates. They must determine

INSET needs from the school INSET co-ordinator, assist in prioritizing and satisfy themselves that the INSET provision required relates to the school development plan, or that it is being expressed as a priority jointly by two or more schools in a group or cluster. Then, having provided the particular INSET activity, was it successful? Was it what was needed? Each of these stages presents difficulties for both schools and teacher advisors; difficulties that will increase rather than ease as the full implications of LMS are felt. Then schools will have to relate INSET plans and priorities to their overall development plan, decide initiatives, discuss these with LEA advisory teams or private sector competitors, and pay for them. For schools, a big problem will be deciding whether they are able to afford the cost of investing in long-term staff development, in keeping with their long-term goals, as opposed to the more pressing and immediate demands of books and maintenance. For LEA advisory teams, the big dilemma will be whether to continue under the wing of an LEA or to operate independently as a reconstituted body, neither tied to LEA boundaries nor restricted in their scope to schools.

The third problem area for consideration is the continuing work of the education welfare officer or education social worker (EWO and ESW). Hitherto this has been a service provided by LEAs in which the EWO or ESW has worked closely with the schools to ensure that any child presenting attitudinal, behavioural or attendance problems could be helped and the home's support enlisted to ensure a consistent, happy and effective school education. With the advent of LMS and the disbursement of LEA funds to schools, doubts have been cast in many LEAs as to the nature and extent of the welfare services they should provide. The doubts centre on whether they should maintain some semblance of the service they have been operating in the hope that schools would want to purchase it. But, with the caution now being exercised in schools over the danger of over-spending, it is likely that most schools faced with the overriding demands of the National Curriculum would regard expenditure on 'welfare' as a low priority, however reluctantly. If this happened the LEA service could not afford to be maintained and would be cut back to the purely statutory responsibility of ensuring that pupils attended school. By the time that schools had found they could manage their budgets and afford a welfare service it might no longer exist, or might have become privatized like similar services in the former Inner London Education Authority (ILEA).

The local authority scene relating to pupil welfare is undergoing changes that are quite important but little noticed. The Children Act 1989 came into force in October 1991 and, while its purpose of ensuring the safety and welfare of children is not primarily aimed at schools, it does require schools to monitor closely the educational progress of children whose parents are divorced and where there are complications. Children of school age 'in care' will need particular attention and reviews of the child's progress will be required, as now, at least every six months.

Peter Smith, writing in the *Times Educational Supplement*, underlined the fact that:

> Failure to attend school will no longer be seen as grounds for seeking a care order. Instead, the work of the education social workers (ESW) or education welfare officers (EWO) can have the backing of the court through an education supervision order.
>
> (Smith 1991)

He also draws attention to the enhanced role that the Act gives the ESW and EWO at a time when their position in some schools is being undermined because of local financial problems and the uncertain future of LEAs.

If schools are to embrace and discharge all their legal responsibilities, the staff and governors will need to be equipped with a wide range of knowledge, skills and understanding. For example, staff development in relation to the demands of curriculum co-ordination (cross-curricular themes), appraisal (teacher and pupil) and mentor roles (newly qualified teachers) will be a major task for any school. With limited resources, and the need to identify and target priorities at an early stage, perhaps the most important task is 'designing and implementing a total staff development plan' (Smith 1991) as the cornerstone of the school development plan.

This must be planned in relation to school policy, and its gradual realization lies at the heart of the implementation of that policy. Implementation may be over an agreed period of several years and should include all staff, governors and associates. The pay-off in terms of team building, corporate endeavour and building a sense of ownership of the policy and programme will be immense. Any alternative is likely to fragment effort, be less cost-effective and ultimately lead to lower morale, poorer performance and a less successful school.

As part of this plan, and as a means of achieving many of its objectives, relations with key outside bodies are crucial, especially those concerned with education and training. While the more established centres of education and training (the universities, polytechnics and colleges of higher education) are all in the process of re-adjusting to re-organization in response to financial stringency, those with a good track record of teacher in-service education remain a priority port of call for any school re-thinking its staff development policy. There has also been a mushrooming of all kinds of training agencies, their growth encouraged by the availability of government and private funds for re-training personnel from business and industry. Most of these specialize in advisory and consultative tasks that would involve co-operating with a school, to identify its training needs, plan a programme and provide appropriate on-site activities.

The difficulty facing the school at this stage is to whom to turn for help and support. Who can be trusted among all these new arrivals on the training scene? One answer in a diminishing LEA presence could well be the nuclear advisory team, in other words, LEA support scenarios 2 or 3, as 'brokers' in facilitating the link between school and dependable private training agencies. This could be an important part of a reduced LEA role along the lines set out earlier in answering LMS support needs. Obviously, the degree of LEA involvement would depend upon the size of the remaining advisory team. But given a group large enough to be of practical help to schools that are undergoing profound and far-reaching changes, this could significantly contribute to their successfully managing their external relations, as well as providing an emerging new role for the former LEAs as 'district educational support services' (DESS). If this were to come about, a small but vigorous DESS could effectively facilitate links between schools and those outside bodies likely to contribute meaningfully and at a fair cost to their development. It seems vital that the LEA, as historically and functionally the most important outside body, should continue its invaluable school support role under whatever title, at least for the foreseeable future.

ACKNOWLEDGEMENTS

The author wishes to acknowledge with gratitude the advice of school colleagues: Claire Buckley, Penny Cole, Sheryl Green, Janis Hill and Peter Moody.

Chapter 6

Links with further education

Michael Snell

'Grace is given of God, but knowledge is bought in the market', wrote the Victorian poet Arthur Hugh Clough (1896). Clough was no stranger to the world of education, occupying at different times in his life the post of principal of University Hall, London, and that of examiner in the Education Office. It may be reasonable to assume, therefore, that he would have found the present marriage of marketing and education both proper and useful. Certainly, his reference to the source of knowledge is one that every headteacher and governor in the post-ERA world of education would do well to mark. As with many phrases that fall easily on the ear, however, it does beg a question or two, the most obvious being 'which market?'.

Among the many current publications available to assist schools with every aspect of their local management of schools (LMS) requirements, including marketing and associated activities, there is a marked lack of reference to further education. A typical chapter heading list will contain extensive guidance on the handling of external relations with feeder schools, community organizations, industry and commerce, the LEA and local councils, but further education attracts little such attention, frequently finding itself combined with 'other schools and colleges'. As the purveyor of goods on a further education market stall, this is a matter for some personal concern, for not only does it perpetuate the Cinderella syndrome of the under-funded and neglected post-sixteen sector, it also pays scant regard to the needs of school-leavers and their adult companions for education, training and retraining for the post-industrial United Kingdom of the 1990s.

The aim of this chapter is to identify that market or market segment that may be described as further education (FE), to suggest why it should be taken account of by the secondary sector and to offer some suggestions as to how it could profitably be addressed.

WHAT IS FE?

My own initiation took place in a college of fashion and clothing technology, followed by a short spell in a technical college, which in turn led to some years of working in a college of technology. After a brief sortie into the world of LEAs, I returned to a senior post in a college of further education and have served latterly for three years as the principal of a tertiary college. I might have added to my experience by working in a higher education institute with a substantial amount of FE work (one such carries the title polytechnic), in a community college or, since 1986, in a city technology college. That very diversity for which the cognoscenti applaud the further education service is, without doubt, responsible for the general and understandable ignorance on the part of both layman and professional of what it actually is.

How, then, can FE be described? The lack of any definitive legislative statement does not help. The last attempt to arrive at a general description was made at the time of the Education Reform Act 1988 when the preponderance of part-time students was cited as being the distinctive feature of the sector. Certainly this is to an extent true today, but the most recent pronouncements of the Secretary of State in the White Paper *Education and Training for the 21st Century* (DES 1991) and the subsequent enactment of the Further and Higher Education Act, 1992, have superseded any such definition. After 1993 it is proposed that all sixth form colleges which at present operate under Schools Regulations should be brought into a new post-sixteen sector. At the same time, the statutory bar on secondary schools admitting part-time students has been removed and the same schools are being strongly urged to diversify the curriculum by the introduction of vocational or work-orientated programmes of study. If all this comes to pass, the myths and mystery of FE will disappear as increasing numbers of schools become involved in the same rich and diverse pattern of work.

The absence of a clear definition for FE is reflected in both its structure and method of operation. The service is essentially pragmatic and entrepreneurial in the way it works. The colleges have learned to react quickly to changing economic and political circumstances and they have, in many senses, created a highly efficient and flexible response to the ever-changing needs of customers. Those customers include school-leavers, employers, the unemployed, minority groups with special learning needs, local authorities and national training agencies. The average FE college has 1,200 full-time students, of average age 16–20, on a range of vocational and academic courses, and a further 2,500 part-time day and/or evening students of all ages on adult education or training programmes. The annual revenue budget will be in the order of £4 million.

There are currently some 425 colleges in England and Wales, and a further 75 in Scotland and Northern Ireland. Most provide a range of courses, but some specialize in such areas as agriculture, art and design, or printing. The old labels of 'evening class' and 'vocational' are belied by the facts. During the last decade there has been a dramatic increase in demand from school-leavers, a reflection of structural changes in secondary education that date from the 1960s and also of social change that has steadily witnessed a growth in student choice at sixteen and a consequent wish for a more adult and negotiated environment in which to learn. As a result, the school sixth form has seen a continuing decline in numbers as the percentage of FE college students taking the traditional academic post-sixteen route of studying for A levels has risen to over 40 per cent. When sixth form colleges merge into the post-1993 FE environment, the new and enlarged FE will be the normal route for the great majority of school-leavers, regardless of whether they are studying for academic or vocational qualifications.

Statistically, the numbers involved are indeed significant. There are now over 3.5 million students working in further education. Of this number, some 450,000 are on full-time programmes and a further 800,000 on part-time day courses. The remainder, in excess of 2.3 million, are following part-time evening courses. Of that 3.5 million, 1.8 million are in FE colleges and 1.7 million in adult education.

Given the present-day entrepreneurialism and pragmatism, the immense diversity of what is available comes as no surprise. A visitor to a typical FE college on an average day is likely to meet large numbers of young people taking both vocational and academic courses. Many will progress to university or polytechnic.

Some students will be involved in pre-vocational programmes and others may be attending from special schools in the area. A visitor to the technology block or a language laboratory may see a group of year 10 or 11 pupils from contributory schools participating in a link course programme. Under the direction of the full-time college sports manager, the sports hall or playing fields may host children from the local primary school while a local music society is preparing the hall for a concert in the evening. In one of the satellite adult education sites there will be adults engaged on part-time leisure and recreation courses, and full-time Access students following an intensive one-year pre-university course preparing them for a first, second or third career, their children in the care of the college day nursery. The flexi-study staff co-ordinator may be conducting a tutorial with one of the growing number of distance learning students, while the day-released youth training or banking and accounting students are studying for their national vocational qualification (NVQ) or other professional qualifications. On the premises of a local employer, a languages lecturer may be providing a tailor-made full-cost course in German for company personnel.

Some colleges engage in operations overseas or manage separately organized companies with special objectives. The introduction of greater independence will add to this already substantial diversity. The current publicity being given to further education far surpasses anything that it has received in the past, adding to the demonstrable success of the colleges to date in extending their contribution and influence throughout the education system. It must therefore be in the interests of the system as a whole to specify the nature of this influence and to adopt appropriate strategies both in response and anticipation.

WHY ESTABLISH RELATIONS WITH FE?

The argument for establishing links between schools and FE can be sustained on two basic grounds: on the need for both efficiency and effectiveness within the education system. These factors will, in turn, almost certainly prove critical in determining which schools are to survive and flourish and which are destined to decline.

The term 'efficiency' is not always welcomed within the education system. One reason is that it has often been seen as a justification for cuts while the real need has been perceived as being for increased expenditure. The word also smacks of managerialism, of which teachers have a healthy suspicion. Whatever the merits of the various points of view, the blunt fact remains that resources for education will remain limited and subject to increasingly careful scrutiny as demand continues to grow. In the case of further education, the recurrent expenditure attributable to the sector for 1991–92 is estimated at over £2 billion, with a further £100 million for capital and equipment investment. This is big business by any standards and the sums involved will be significantly larger for the secondary sector. Certainly, within higher education, the recent trend has been to finance the service more on the basis of a market economy, with funds following recruitment and being competitively bid for by the institutions concerned. The result has been a sharp decline in the real value of a student unit of resource and consequent pressures on individual budgets. There is every reason to believe that similar processes will be adopted in the post-sixteen sector and be extended further down the age range. The price of great independence and freedom for local management will be significantly greater pressure on budgets and a consequent need for careful and efficient management of resources.

The present drive towards greater independence and autonomy for schools is both understandable and exciting. The incentive of cash supplements following acceptance of grant-maintained school (GMS) status is considerable. A sustained and real increase in both revenue and capital resources for education is more problematic and difficult to foresee. The temptation for schools to seek our survival through independence and self-sufficiency is strong, but institutional managers will do well to remember that such an approach is locked irrevocably into the aggressive marketing model of private enterprise. In the simplest of terms, this model rewards the entrepreneurial and publicity-seeking risk taker, while it penalizes those of a less adventurous temperament. For many, such an approach will seem at best inappropriate for the education service. At worst, it will lead to duplication, wasted resources, inaccurate information and reduced quality.

Of one thing we can be certain. The present emphasis on parent (customer) power, added to the individualist principles of local management of schools, will lead to a wide diversity of marketing approaches. The prudent headteacher will adopt a measured policy that is appropriate to the needs of the school and that can be afforded within budget. An approach of this kind may well witness closer links and greater collaboration with other schools, FE and sixth form colleges than is envisaged at present. The experience of higher education, and increasingly that of further education, is that where units of resource are in real decline in the face of growing student numbers the need to find less expensive methods of delivery and to make the most efficient use of them becomes paramount. For schools, FE colleges may be a future resource of real significance.

FE colleges often control significant quantities of advanced capital equipment in high-tech environments on extensive sites. These facilities frequently include open-access information technology centres with computer hardware and software of a standard comparable with that found in industry. They might also include engineering workshops with heavy machinery and state-of-the-art computer-controlled machines. Accompanying this is the expertise, in the form of trained staff, and the development of new techniques and methods of delivery. In the latter case, the emergence of flexible learning systems has been of particular note. The shared use and selective purchase of these resources by schools has only been developed in a limited way to date and, in many cases, has been inhibited by lack of knowledge of their potential. The successful exploitation of opportunities that now exist for schools to open up vocational courses for young people will depend upon collaboration with FE colleges. Without it, the cost of delivery in the form of appropriate technology will be too great. How much improved would the delivery of the National Curriculum also be were these opportunities to be grasped?

In the same way that the growth in student numbers entering higher education has led to extensive franchising of courses to the FE sector, so we might expect to see forward-looking secondary schools take up the challenge. A strong argument for understanding and linking with FE therefore exists in the principles of sound business management based on a medium-term view of the economic cycle rather than on the view of the short-term speculator.

The argument for a more effective service is one that should be closer to the educationist's heart. It has led to the broad acceptance of the general principles of the National Curriculum, even though there may be heated disagreement about the detail. The measure of the UK's economic, political and social success as a post-industrial nation is now more directly linked to the education system than at any time in the past. In this respect the national league tables indicating the number of young people who remain in education after the statutory school-leaving age make bleak reading. Recent figures released by the Office of Population Censuses and Statistics (OPCS) indicate that, at 70 per cent, the staying-on rate of those aged 16–18 in the UK lags behind most of the member nations of the EC. A comparable rate for Belgium and the Netherlands is 90 per cent. The proportion of those aged 18–24 in higher education in the UK is under 10 per cent, compared with nearly 22 per cent in France, Belgium, Germany, Spain and Denmark. This may be attributed to a number of factors, but there can be little doubt that the lack of coherence in our system, matched by inadequate continuity and progression, are responsible to a significant degree. There is, therefore, a challenge now confronting all parts of the service to work towards a major improvement, which will require closer collaboration rather than more intense competition.

Despite the initial conservative reaction on the part of many teachers to the TVEI programme, there are few who would now doubt its value in raising many central issues. Curricular continuity at sixteen is, to a considerable extent, dependent upon the examination system and in this respect the influence of schools is limited. However, the management of progression from GCSE to either A level or vocational courses is very much within the control of institutions. The establishing of TVEI consortia of schools and colleges in 1983 brought to the surface, for the first time in many areas, the discontinuity and fragmentation that have built up. In many areas, 11–18 comprehensive schools and FE and sixth form colleges jostled together uncomfortably for the first time around a table which had, as its main agenda item, the needs of the students. It took many months for trust to be established and even then the spectre of falling rolls remained a shadow over many of the initiatives. Now, in more enlightened areas, we see the sharing of expertise in the form of exchanged teachers, the development of link courses and a marked improvement in attitudes towards adult learners. Recent proposals mean that long-established barriers to continuity are to be progressively removed; schools will be allowed to recruit part-time students openly, both within mainstream classes and also through adult education programmes. The notion of education as a continuous process is one that has long held sway in a number of European countries while our own approach has stayed with the idea of a one-off win or lose experience to be had at a particular age. Learning as a life-long, universal experience is to be welcomed, but it can only develop in this way if the institutions providing the opportunities work closely together – from infant through primary, secondary, tertiary and higher education.

Marketing as a systematic approach to the development of FE was developed in the first half of the 1980s. It arose as the result of official concern expressed by the Audit Commission and by HM Inspectorate about the lack of responsiveness and effective promotion within the service. The concern coincided with demographic predictions that suggested a dramatic decline in student numbers through the 1990s. The considerable resistance with which the new approach was initially met was therefore tempered by the real prospect of redundancies following widespread closure of colleges. Colleges are now booming in response to a rapidly rising staying-on rate and to a burgeoning demand from the new market segments that have been opened up. What was originally a problem of supply has quickly become one of demand, and most marketing managers within FE now consider their prime task as being to manage demand at the highest level of quality rather than any problems of student numbers.

The secondary sector could now be facing a very similar situation to that of FE in the 1980s. The transferability of the marketing model is unproblematic and the prizes are significant. The major advances are made through changed attitudes that follow acceptance of the model. These new attitudes accept the marketplace as being competitive, but not necessarily in the profit-making sense, and they identify and place the needs of the customer first, whether parent or pupil. The question remains: how does the school set about the task?

ESTABLISHING LINKS WITH FE

Elsewhere in this book (Chapter 1) a consideration of planning models for the organization of external relations in schools has emphasized the development of an overall external relations strategy, with the willing change of attitude on the part of staff and, indeed, pupils as its central objective. Such a strategy will acknowledge the need for a systematic approach to planning and a recognition that organizational structures may have to be altered. It will also recognize the need to support the plan with real resources. Central to this is understanding the external relations structure of partner organizations. In the case of FE colleges, it is now common for the marketing function to be placed at the centre of activity under the control of a senior member of the management team, who may in turn be responsible for a team of marketing staff with specific business-related objectives to achieve. Many of these will relate to mainstream educational objectives that are of immediate relevance to schools. Clarifying these links and building on them must be part of the external relations audit and marketing plan.

The practical outcomes of using a framework of this kind may not be predictable; therein lies one of the main attractions of an approach that invites new and imaginative ways of thinking and that can mobilize teams of staff in the best interests of the school. An enabling plan involves all staff in contributing to the welfare of the organization. As far as relating to FE is concerned, it will lead to the introduction and/or expansion of link-course programmes, shared use of premises and collaboration in work exchange programmes or trips abroad. It will see the growth of shared teaching and assessment, the emergence of franchising and, most important of all, a more coherent curriculum for pupils and students. The present debate about the applicability of 'quality' models to education – whether BS5750 or total quality management – will accelerate and certainly permeate into the school sector. Schools will find that a marketing philosophy will prepare them well for the reflective style and planning methods required.

'The intellectual has never felt kindly toward the marketplace; to him it has always been a place of vulgar men and base motives' (Stigler 1963). The experience of the world of FE is that, far from proving a debasing activity, skilful marketing has provided a vital and liberating force that has benefited colleges and students alike. Progressive schools will wish to enjoy a similar experience.

Chapter 7

Links with higher education

Nicholas Foskett

THE EDUCATIONAL LINK – PATRONAGE OR PARTNERSHIP?

Higher education and schools have traditionally been viewed as the opposite ends of a broad spectrum of provision within the UK education system. At one pole, the schools have provided basic education for all up to the minimum school-leaving age, at which point the majority leave the system with a feeling of release and relief. At the other pole, higher education has provided a narrow, usually academic or professionally vocational, education to small numbers of students selected through a discriminatory system designed to facilitate exclusion. The traditional control of public examinations by boards under the auspices of the universities with university teachers playing a dominant role in establishing content and style, meant that the curriculum throughout secondary education was much influenced by the universities' entrance requirements. Yet the relationship between schools and higher education has always been a distant one. Control and influence were exerted largely in one direction, with schools submitting passively to the needs of higher education and gratuitously seeking patronage, and hence community credibility, in providing small numbers of selected students to the system, gaining good examination results for a wider group and recruiting graduates from prestigious institutions to the teaching staff.

The culture of education in the UK has seen a sea change over the last three decades, however, providing a stimulus to a changing relationship between higher education and schools. First, higher education has slowly moved away from its narrowly élitist position. With a first stimulus from the Robbins Report (1963) and the expansion of the university sector in the mid-1960s, access has been broadened, a trend accelerated by the growth of public sector higher education in the 1970s and 1980s. This has provided a wider range of institutions, courses and styles to the system. In addition, the fear of declining numbers in the HE entry cohort through to 1995, as a result of birth rate changes in the mid-1970s, stimulated higher education to seek alternative ways of recruiting. The growth of the Access movement (Parry 1989, Tuckett 1990), the investment in sophisticated schools liaison and marketing services, and the development of innovations such as part-time and modular courses with credit-transfer mechanisms (Toyne 1990) were symptomatic of this pressure. It has become clear, however, that recruitment in the 1990s is not the problem once feared. In part this is because the reduction in the age cohort through to 1995 is almost entirely due to reductions in birth rate among socio-economic classes 4 and 5, which traditionally showed little uptake of HE places. In reality the birth rate in the higher socio-economic classes had actually risen, so enhancing competition for places. Allied to this have been clear changes in the numbers of school pupils seeking HE entry, so that the numbers of first-year full-time undergraduates grew by 36 per cent from 1979–89 (DES 1991b). In addition, government has sought to expand participation in higher education rapidly throughout the 1990s, a policy that should lead to nearly one-third of those aged 18–19 entering higher education by the year 2000 (DES 1991b). Inevitably, this has resulted in a challenge to the power of selectivity for higher education institutions, and has passed to the schools a much greater role in and responsibility for influencing the flow of students into higher education. Higher education selectors are still the gatekeepers, but the gates have been widened and additional gates provided.

Second, the control of the curriculum has moved into the hands of the schools and away from higher education, and three pressures have been important in this process. The introduction of the Certificate of Secondary Education (CSE) was a first step in modifying the academic curriculum to meet the needs of the majority of pupils. Courses were still essentially in academic subjects, but new assessment styles and school-designed Mode 3 syllabuses stimulated a change in classroom practice to a more pupil-centred, skills-based style. This trend was extended to the whole of the 14–16 age range with the introduction of the General Certificate of Secondary Education (GCSE) in 1985, which provided a unitary system for school examination at 16 plus. Allied to this has been the transformation of post-sixteen courses to provide a more appropriate, skills-based education with a wider range of assessment methods (for example, the 16–19 Geography Project). Teachers and schools are now at the helm of the school curriculum.

A second facet has been the rise of vocationalism. The growth of Business and Technician Education Council (BTEC) qualifications in the colleges of further education has posed a challenge to higher education which they have resisted staunchly until recently. The equivalence of such qualifications with more traditional ones from within the system has met only half-hearted support from, in particular, the university sector, except where competition for declining numbers of applicants made it necessary, in areas such as engineering. More successful has been the Technical and Vocational Education Initiative (TVEI) (Gleeson 1989). This was established in 1982 to broaden the curriculum in schools to include technical and vocational aspects. How far the scheme's popularity reflected its input of resources into schools or its opportunity for curriculum innovation is hard to gauge, but it certainly had the effect of shifting attitudes to the curriculum away from the narrow academic view.

A third facet has been the debate over the 16–19 curriculum. The narrowness of the traditional curriculum, with its study of three academic Advanced level (A level) subjects, has been challenged almost since the inception of A levels in 1951, with demands for a broadening of the curriculum – the N and F proposals (Schools Council 1973) and the Higginson Report (DES 1988a), for example. In all cases the government's response was to reject the proposals and retain A levels as the 'gold standard' of the education system. Instead, broadening was initiated by the introduction of Advanced Supplementary (AS) examinations. Uptake of AS has been slow, and this reflects a natural inertia in the system, compounded by pressures in schools simultaneously to develop GCSE and the new National Curriculum. More particularly, however, it reflects a fear about the acceptability of the 2A plus 2AS combination for higher education entry by parents, pupils and schools, despite extensive assurances from higher education that it recognizes their value as entry qualifications (Wake 1989). Further broadening of the curriculum has been proposed in terms of the availability of mixed academic and vocational courses as foreseen by the government's White Paper, *Education and Training for the 21st Century* (DES 1991b). Such developments are still seen by many as simply tinkering at the periphery of a fundamentally flawed system driven by the academic requirements for traditional university courses.

These curriculum changes have loosened the grip of higher education in dictating the school curriculum. What has been the reaction of HE? The changes are clearly welcomed and encouraged by the formal HE representative bodies, including the Standing Conference on University Entrance (SCUE), with its long-term perspective of enhanced HE participation (Wake 1989). Participation in Access schemes and the development of franchising arrangements whereby early parts of HE courses are taught in other institutions with a guarantee of progression to HE are clear demonstrations of this (Parry and Wake 1990). Within the informal environments support is less obvious, however, where conservatism and the slow pace at which the rapid innovations in schools are being understood mitigate against support.

SCHOOLS AND HIGHER EDUCATION – A WAY FORWARD

It is clear, therefore, that the links between schools and higher education have changed. The relationship has become one that is capable of much greater management from within schools. Partnership is slowly replacing patronage as the guiding concept at the school–higher education interface. We can examine two aspects of this relationship to identify the possible organizational response from within schools:

1 the educational progression of school students into higher education and the management of HE advisory, application, recruitment and placement activities – **the student link**; and
2 the relationship with initial teacher training institutions in higher education in terms of supporting their training function, recruiting new staff and providing continuing education for existing staff and support in institutional development and management – **the professional staffing link**.

The student link

The recruitment of students into colleges, polytechnics and universities is a major self-sustaining industry. In the early pre-Robbins days of matching small numbers of applicants to a small number of institutions, there developed a group of careers teachers whose inside knowledge and range of contacts across the boundary in higher education ensured a smooth passage for the students they knew. The system was *ad hoc* in character, with little serious attempt to ensure a close match between student need and course provision or recruitment in HE. The establishment of UCCA for university entrance, the Central Register and Clearing House (CRCH) for entry to teacher-training courses and PCAS for polytechnic entrance introduced some element of organized decision-making and selection to applications.

Centralized systems are clearly necessary to cope with 400,000 applications for entry into higher education each year, and ensure, within reasonable limits, the equitable treatment of all applicants. Until recently, though, the interests of the clients, both students and schools, seemed secondary to the interests of higher education. Typical was the priority system that UCCA retained until 1988, which required applicants to place their five choices of course and institution in order of preference. This device was used by most universities to facilitate their selection process by paying relatively little attention to applications that placed them as fourth or fifth choice. The removal of the priority system meant that universities were forced to abandon many of their selection processes such as formal interviews because of the need to consider all applicants. While this may have reduced some of the personal contact for applicants, it meant that far more applicants ended up with a real choice of institution. The common application process – in which students can apply for virtually all higher education courses on a single form – introduced for 1992 makes the process easier for both students and their advisors in schools.

In considering the managerial implications of the HE admissions process for schools, it is necessary to take three perspectives: that of the students, that of the schools and that of the HE institutions. Unfortunately, while there are some goals common to the three groups, it is easy to identify potential conflicts.

The goal of higher-education institutions is unambiguous. They seek to recruit an adequate number of students to fill their courses, and strive to ensure that their students are among the most able in their field. This process ensures academic respectability, financial security and, in the long term, the achievement of good results in performance indicators such as graduate employment record and average A level score of entrants. This presents a fairly harsh view, in that most institutions, departments and admissions staff have a much more humane and liberal view of the process. There is a genuine concern to ensure that students make choices that are wise and in their own long-term interests, and that some social engineering occurs through the manipulation of numbers of entrants from minority or disadvantaged groups. However, the admissions process is operated by HE to ensure that the ultimate aims are achieved in an increasingly competitive market.

Since the mid-1980s the undergraduate marketing process has become more sophisticated. Virtually all HE institutions employ a schools liaison officer, with responsibilities for organizing a range of recruitment activities. These include open days for potential applicants, the provision of speakers to schools on all aspects of HE life and applications, the production of marketing literature, including prospectuses and other materials, and attendance at the growing number of higher education conventions where HE institutions are invited to meet potential applicants. While there are many altruistic aspects of this work, the activities are substantially those of marketing officers in commerce. The aim is the attraction of potential applicants, and the conversion of offers of places into firm acceptances.

If we examine two of the tools of HE marketers the issues will become clear. The most important aspect of HE promotion is literature, the prime source of information and motivation to apply for over 70 per cent of applicants (Foskett 1988), and many institutions have invested in the advice of professional designers to produce a stimulating and user-friendly product. The image the literature portrays is certainly the truth, but whether it is the whole truth may be questionable. A second tool of the trade is the higher education convention, where many institutions will provide a stand and a representative to answer questions from and provide information to potential applicants. The conventions are, without doubt, of enormous value for potential applicants who are some way through the decision-making process of selecting courses and institutions in that they enable them to meet representatives of their short list at first hand. For less aware students there seems little virtue in the window shopping that the conventions provide, as they compound the information overload that they may experience.

For the schools, the aims are much more student focused, although not devoid of consideration of other factors, and the support system for students in making HE choices is highly sophisticated. A typical process will begin in year 1 of a two-year course, with the provision of advice to students in groups, or even as individuals, on the options beyond the age of eighteen. Visits to a local HE institution may be arranged to get a feel for HE, or speakers, either academics or students, may be invited to provide an insight into life at university, polytechnic or college. The formal process of application will also involve counselling on making choices, filling in application forms and interview methods, with detailed guidance on the sources of useful information. Part of the formal process involves the completion of a reference by the school, which may include a critical review of the application.

A number of issues might be identified in this process. First, it provides a bureaucratic structure which may not be in the student's best interest. The scale of the problem for the schools, particularly for large institutions, is the reason for this, but it may mean that each student receives little guidance and advice.

Second, the scale of the advisory problem is huge. There are at present in the UK over 15,000 undergraduate courses available in over 300 institutions (Heap 1990) and it is an intractable information problem for the adviser, let alone the student, to cope with. The role of the advisory service must be to ensure that students develop a model of information retrieval and decision-making that will result in appropriate decisions, rather than suggesting particular courses to particular students. A useful model of this sort can be found in Foskett and Foskett (1989). Obtaining objective information may be a particular problem. Most advice to applicants in schools comes from subject teachers, rather than careers or HE advisors. This process assumes that subject teachers have insight into the relative merits of all institutions that provide their subject at degree level, and can give objective advice on the merits of their own subject as a discipline for study compared with other traditional fields and vocational areas. This seems an optimistic hope.

Finally, schools themselves are in the business of recruitment and one of their performance indicators to parents of potential recruits is HE entry. There can be little doubt that schools seek to maximize HE entry, and will push pupils towards those courses and institutions that might be considered particularly prestigious in the eyes of parents. How far does this conflict with the needs of the student?

The students' needs in the process are clear. Their single opportunity within the HE marketplace requires both the provision of skills in accessing information and decision-making, and also the availability of objective advice. The evidence suggests that sound decisions are being made, in that the drop-out rate in UK HE is less than 10 per cent. However, in 1990 the results of a survey by PCAS and HEIST (Keen and Higgins 1990) suggested a surprising ignorance of HE among sixth formers in schools. The results showed that '31.2% of sixth formers at the end of their course said they did not know enough about higher education to make a sound choice' (Keen and Higgins 1990) and this related particularly to knowledge about courses and institutions outside the university sector. This view has been confirmed by Roberts and Higgins (1992), whose research demonstrates that few higher education students were satisfied with the advice they received in making their choices, and 20 per cent of entrants sought no advice from careers advisors and teachers.

How might the tripartite relationship considered here be enhanced and managed for the benefit of all concerned? The major conflict is between the need for a system that can operate to deal with applications on a large scale, and the personalizing of the service to the individual applicant. Without major resource inputs into the system it may be that the current balance between the two facets of the problem is an appropriate one. The present system usually manages to provide both a source of expertise on accessing information – the careers teacher or HE advisor – and a source of personal support – the individual tutor or teacher. Problems arise for the student when either oversteps the limits of his or her expertise. Clearly of importance is increasing the awareness among applicants of their role in the selection market and the pressures to which they will be subjected. Only then can the goodwill, co-operation and real expertise of HE be recognized through the marketing smokescreen the students will experience. There is clearly a need for in-service training for all those working with pre-HE students, to maintain their awareness of the application process, the nature of HE and the complexities of the decision-making process for students. This may be facilitated by providing a forum for continuing dialogue between schools or colleges and higher education through school–HE liaison groups like those found in some universities, for example, Aston and Southampton, or through a twinning process. This involves admissions tutors from higher education forming close ties with relevant heads of subject departments in schools, to enable the sharing of expertise and insights to occur.

The professional staffing link

In most countries, teachers are required to undertake a period of professional training before being admitted into the work-force, and the system of training that is of necessity established to support this means that there is a continuing relationship between schools or colleges and HE. The provision of initial teacher training (ITT) by HE, whether in the form of brief postgraduate courses or longer undergraduate or non-graduate certificate or diploma courses, maintains an obvious facet of the external relations of schools through two links: the provision of periods of teaching practice where trainees work in schools alongside experienced and qualified teachers, and the recruitment of new permanent staff to schools from among the cohort of newly qualified teachers (NQTs). This is extended by the links that occur through in-service training for practising teachers.

The formal management of this link with HE has usually been divided in schools into two facets. The professional tutor, first advocated by the James Report (DES 1972), tends to have responsibility for links relating to education and training. This will include liaison with ITT institutions about the placement, supervision and assessment of trainees, and the monitoring and management of the staff development programme. The second role, that of recruitment, falls within the ambit of headteachers and, since the Education Reform Act 1988, of the governing body. This describes the formal relationship only, however, in that the day-to-day contact in both areas tends to be between individual tutors in HE and either class teachers, in primary schools, or heads of department, in secondary schools, to whom will fall the task of supervising the work of student teachers as line managers and whose personal links with HE tutors may well be a primary means of attracting applicants for posts. It is clearly important that both these links are nurtured by schools and the HE institutions for their mutual benefit.

For the HE institution, the role of liaison cannot be left to chance. At the formal level there is a need to designate someone to have school link responsibilities within the management of both initial and in-service training. An average Postgraduate Certificate in Education Course (PGCE) might include placements for 200 students in some 100 schools; for a Bachelor of Education course (BEd) there might be 500 students in 250 schools. For INSET provision the recruitment may be regional or national in scale, and the number of schools involved proportionately larger. If the liaison is to be a proper interactive relationship, rather than a purely mechanical administrative one, there is a clear need for a single point of contact in the institution. On a day-to-day basis the ambassadorial role of all HE tutors visiting schools needs to be seen as important. They are the continuing point of contact, with the purpose of each visit not simply to see the students, but to provide a link with the school on other issues.

From both sides of the relationship, if the link is to flourish a number of liaison and training issues need to be addressed. An appropriate model might include the following.

1 Annual consultation at a formal level between schools and HE institutions to discuss issues of mutual concern.
2 For ITT, the provision of training in mentor and supervisory skills by the HE institution for senior school staff and line managers.
3 Interchange of staff between schools and HE institutions. This occurs at present, to some extent, through the arrangements made to satisfy the requirement of the Council for the Accreditation of Teacher Education (CATE) that ITT tutors spend one term every five years undertaking 'recent and relevant' teaching experience (DES 1989). It seems, however, that this involvement of HE staff with schools is rarely seen by either participant in the arrangement as an opportunity for organizational or staff development.
4 Closer links between schools and HE institutions in the design, organization and delivery of both ITT and INSET programmes. The pressure for this is clear and a number of responses have developed. These include the mentor system, in use in the PGCE programmes at the University of Oxford and Sussex University.

This system links the PGCE very closely with a small number of schools which both contribute to the design and teaching of the course and also take students as 'interns' for the whole course. The students' time is split between school and institution each week. The mentors are the school staff with responsibility for the students' programme in school. The advantages of integration and student involvement in a single school are clear, but balanced against this is a concern that the students experience only a limited insight into education by links with only one school, and risk socialization into the culture of that one school rather than into that of the whole education system. Furthermore, the administrative demands on the staff in school in addition to their normal teaching/administrative load might militate against a truly effective support system.

An alternative is the 'teaching school' model, similar in format to the 'teaching hospital' for training doctors. This sees the development of close links between an HE institution and a small number of schools, but with a flexible movement of staff and students between the institutions. Students will gain an insight into a number of schools and might undertake teaching practice in more than one. Staff from the HE institution will contribute to teaching in the schools and vice versa, and the level of counselling and student support within the group will be higher than may be possible in a large number of schools. Models of this sort have yet to be put into operation, although DES/DFE proposals (DES 1992) see this structure emerging for the training of secondary phase teachers in the UK. While such schemes would seem to combine the virtues of appropriate professional education with in-school training on a continuing basis, it is not clear how far cost and the resistance of parents to having their children in such schools would be a problem. In addition, it is clear that if teachers are to receive more than a simple mechanistic training, constrained by the views, philosophy and day-to-day needs of a single school, then there is an upper limit to the amount of time that should be spent in schools on such a course. The sharing of ideas, time for reflection and contact with both a broad range of approaches and innovation need a significant place in the course. Proposals for 80 per cent of such courses to be school based would seem to militate against this.

A further area of linkage in this field relates to the induction of newly qualified teachers (NQTs) into the profession. The 1988 report, *The New Teacher in School* (HMI 1988), is highly critical of liaison between HE and schools in this sphere. It suggests that a system of profiling in ITT may be a way of providing a detailed insight into a new teacher's individual professional development needs. Many higher education institutions are actively developing profiling systems to match this need.

Schools might benefit from proactively seeking these links with HE institutions through a senior member of staff. A recent unpublished survey (Foskett 1991) of schools hosting teaching practice students from the School of Education at Southampton University suggests that most schools consider that the benefits of such links outweigh the problems that may arise from supervising teaching practice (TP) students. In particular, the chance to access the new, energetic insights of students, to provide a new stimulus to pupils' work, and the opportunity to evaluate current practice in the school through the evaluation of students are significant benefits. Only where weak students are present in the TP are significant problems identified. In particular, the synergy of a continuing relationship with one or two HE education departments, with the possibility of joint appointments and staff exchanges, may be seen as a valuable pay-off in curriculum terms for the school. With changing approaches to teacher training, schools will not see themselves as the minor partner in the relationship, as some do, but as an equal partner in a symbiotic link with the institution.

A number of current trends in schools may support this move. The delegation to schools of INSET funds under local management of schools means that they have much more control over the provision of INSET, including award-bearing courses such as MA(Ed) and M Ed programmes, and can negotiate with individual HE institutions to provide appropriate courses or appropriate course structures. Second, the introduction of the licensed teacher schemes, and to a lesser extent the articled teacher schemes, means that schools may be engaged in negotiating appropriate support for such teachers. Third, having close links with training institutions must give some advantage in gaining access to NQTs for teaching posts.

CONCLUSION

It is clear that the relationship between schools and higher education is evolving to a much closer partnership (Duffy 1990). This means that the management challenge is changing from that of providing a purely responsive system in the school to that of having a more interactive relationship. Perhaps it is possible to see the development of a cluster or pyramid system in local areas which reflects the developments linking primary and secondary schools and, in some cases, tertiary institutions. In these new clusters the apex of the pyramid would be the local HE institutions, which increasingly look towards their local schools and colleges for a supply of students, and thus extend the already local system of provision of ITT and INSET.

A number of pressures might be identified as leading towards this. The rapid expansion of HE through the next two decades will produce much larger institutions, much more flexible course provision and a situation where a much higher proportion of those aged eighteen and above will continue into HE. Financial constraints on students, with an increase in the proportion of those who are self-funding to some extent, will also produce two trends: more part-time students and more students who seek to live at home while studying. All these pressures will undoubtedly lead to a localization of HE provision, where HE institutions increasingly serve their local community for most higher education and are perhaps centres of national recruitment only in one or two areas of excellence. This should mean that schools no longer see HE as a distant cousin residing in another part of the country, but as a close family member who lives in the local area. From the other side of the relationship it should lead to an increasing awareness by HE of its role within the whole education system and its involvement with the local community.

Part 3

Links with the community

Chapter 8

Liaising with parents

Ina Hanford

Liaison between schools and the parents of their pupils is based on a well-founded tradition. The usual methods by which schools and parents liaise include meetings for parents of prospective pupils, parents' consultative meetings and individual interviews. Many schools have parent–teacher associations (PTAs) and enjoy parental help in the classroom. More recently, governors and schools have worked together to produce an annual report for parents and to meet them in order to discuss the report.

The benefits to schools of good links with parents have never seriously been in question. A constructive working relationship benefits the school and the child. One of the prime aims of the Education Act 1986 (No 2) was to promote an enhanced partner-ship between schools, governors, LEA and parents; and parents now constitute a large group on governing bodies. Prior to 1986, the Education Act 1980 gave parents the right to express a prefer-ence for a school, but with qualifications that denied absolute freedom. The notion of giving power to parents was supported by advisors on government educational policy in the 1980s:

> We have moved a long way to restoring the rightful, central place to parents and children, but so far we have refused to accept the logic of that in the management of schools. In any other enterprise it is the clients, the customers, whose demands and needs have to be met by the suppliers if they are to stay in business.
>
> (Sexton 1990: 17)

Whether one supports the marketplace concept or not is really now academic. The reality is that the terms 'partnership' and 'liaison' have taken on a new urgency in the 1990s in the context of open enrolment and formula funding. It is no longer sufficient to consider the purely educational and social benefits accruing from good home–school relations; rather, it has become essential for schools to gain parental interest and commitment, as failure to do so will probably result in a declining roll, fewer funds and a continuing downward spiral for the school. However, while much has been written about the effects of entering such a spiral, no blueprint exists that schools can adopt in order to ensure their long-term success. An illustration of this may be seen in the adoption of a marketing perspective in schools, which has encouraged focusing on specific strengths and virtues in the school. Yet the dangers of such excellent but narrow specialisms are all too real. The school in a catchment area with a socio-economic mix that proclaims its excellence in special needs provision, or music or some other sphere, may find that it appeals only to a small percentage of possible clients, to its detriment. A more generalized mission would appeal to most parents, such as:

1 a constant striving for excellence by the headteacher and staff;
2 confidence by staff in the school's functions and procedures;
3 a constructive working relationship with parents; and
4 stability, sensitivity and clarity of purpose.

What should be the role of parents within the school? MacBeth (1989) considers parents as the legal clients of a school and as stakeholders in their child's education. Parents have a legal duty to ensure the education of their children, according to Section 36 of the Education Act 1944. It is, however, the duty of others – government, LEA and school – to ensure that the means are provided whereby a child can receive an education. The parent enters into no legal obligation with the school and makes an agreement only on such matters as attendance and adherence to rules. The onus for provision rests largely with these other organizations; the onus for liaison goes beyond the bare legal requirements and is an essential part of the management function of schools.

This chapter will consider the two main management challenges inherent in the concept of liaison with parents:

1 the statutory obligation on schools to transmit information and the nature of that information;
2 the creation of an appropriate and effective structure for liaison.

PARENTS, INFORMATION AND THE LAW

What information has to be transmitted to or may be required to be seen by parents? Clearly the most pertinent areas currently are those relating to pupil records, pupil reports and documents such as the school prospectus.

Pupil records

The governing body is responsible for maintaining a record on every child on the school register. Parents and children over sixteen have a right to see the record within fifteen school days of a written request to the governing body. Records made before September 1989 are exempt from the regulations and disclosure would depend therefore on the LEA or governing body's policy (Education Reform Act 1988 (Section 22); Education (School Records) Regulations 1989; and DES Circular 17/89). Schools already keep records in respect of each child and update them annually with new copies of school reports and other achievements covering aspects of the whole development of the child. Certain information may not be disclosed, however, including anything that could identify another pupil. Similarly, anything that could cause serious harm to the pupil or another person may not be disclosed. References are confidential to appropriate personnel and may not be disclosed, as are reports relating to actual or alleged child abuse, or those written for juvenile courts. Anything relating to ethnic data may not be disclosed.

There are clear messages already in this one aspect of the management of school records. While the internal management of the process may entail nothing more than the organization of administrative procedures – files to be checked and any non-disclosable material withdrawn – there are clear implications for time management, for awareness raising among staff who have access to pupil information, for security arrangements and for the whole nature of liaison. The latter depends on the extent of the school's willingness on the one hand, to build a close working partnership with parents or, on the other, simply to fulfil the letter of the law. Whatever the staff's personal views, it seems that we ought to be in the business of being open and responsive to parent clients.

Reporting on pupil progress

Schools have to report to parents on their child's progress at least once a year, by 31 July for pupils in years 1–10, and by 30 September for all pupils in year 11. Reports must give information about National Curriculum programmes of study and the child's attainment levels within them. Particulars of results in any public examinations must be included in the report, and the later date of 30 September for year 11 pupils allows the incorporation of such particulars. The National Curriculum does not, of course, constitute the whole curriculum, and pupils' work and achievement in activities that form part of the whole-school curriculum should also be included in the report (Education Reform Act 1988 (Section 22); Education (Individual Pupils' Achievements) (Information) Regulations 1990; DES Circular 8/90). In this field the legislation is contradictory. Both the Education Reform Act and the subsequent regulations and circular place emphasis on the importance of full and broad reporting of achievement, such as that conveyed in the record of achievement, yet they do not introduce the necessary legislation to place such full and broad reporting on a statutory footing.

There are several issues for school managers to consider here. First, the process leading to the production of records of achievement is time-consuming and costly. Second, given that the school report is eagerly awaited and analysed, it is worth investing time in establishing what type of report parents wish to receive. One may be forgiven for asking just how meaningful or useful to parents is the subjective written ramble that now characterizes some report documents. However, if a school transfers to the statement bank method of reporting, the administration processes are eased but the pupil goes home clutching a report that places his or her attainment in neat but impersonal boxes. Careful management of the process of reporting, in consultation with parents and beyond the bare legal requirements, will do much to create effective liaison.

A prime objective of the National Curriculum is to achieve some measure of national standardization, and schools have received from the DES/DFE a sample school report form that is proposed as a possible model for the annual report to parents. The sample includes a section entitled 'Recommendations for action by parents' and offers the opportunity for discussion between parents and teacher.

Records of achievement and reports relating to the National Curriculum will pose challenges to schools in communicating with parents. While LEAs have published short, reader-friendly digests on records of achievement for parental consumption, there seems to be little continuity of the process of explanation – a task that falls to school management teams concerned about liaison. This task will be all the more relevant in the future, when explanation will be required of possible anomalies in reports. The record of achievement emphasizes the positive aspects of pupil development; SATs and attainment levels will show actual achievement and the two will not necessarily be synonymous. Both will require careful explanation to parents.

Reporting on broader issues

Parents may be concerned primarily about the development of their child, but they may wish to find out as much information as possible about the school as an organization. Hanford (1990) has examined the information needs expressed by parents. These included a wish to know:

1 more about the curriculum;
2 more about examination results, in a reader-friendly way;
3 about the changes in education;
4 about the new role of the governing body;
5 about the provision for areas of study beyond the National Curriculum;
6 how to assist their child in coursework requirements;
7 about teaching methods; and
8 about pastoral care policy.

Other research supports the views expressed in this survey. The National Consumer Council (1977) commissioned a Gallup poll on parents' attitudes to schools. According to this, 39 per cent of parents said they were dissatisfied with the amount of information they received about teaching methods and subject choices. Nearly a quarter felt they would be interfering if they went to the school uninvited. In 1978 an investigation undertaken by Nottingham University (Nottingham University School of Education 1978) found that most schools concentrated on purely informative matter in written communications between home and school and a limited number encouraged parents to participate, although in a rather bleak style. Research at Sussex University (East Sussex County Council/University of Sussex 1979) found that parents expressed a strong wish for information and avidly read all they received; they were given very little about the curriculum of a kind that would help them support their child's learning. Their views are expressed in the following resolution from the National Consumer Congress:

> This Congress requests the National Consumer Council to urge government and education authorities . . . to promote all forms of partnership with parents . . . to ensure that help in communicating with parents forms part of the initial and in-service training of every teacher . . . to research and disseminate methods of communication with parents including the least confident and to spread good practice.

> (National Consumer Council 1986a: 8)

The school prospectus

Perhaps the major avenue for liaison between a school and the parents of prospective pupils is the school prospectus. The legal requirements for its content are quite precise (Education Act 1980 (Section 8); Education (School Information) Regulations 1981; Education Reform Act 1988 (Section 22); and Education (School Curriculum and Related Information) Regulations 1989). While the list of requirements is daunting, some of the information may be summarized and parents referred to other sources for further details. Times of publication are clearly specified: primary and special school prospectuses must be published in advance of the school year to which they relate, while middle and secondary school prospectuses must be published at least six weeks before parents have to apply for admission to the school, or at least six weeks before parents have to express a preference for a school, whichever is the earlier. Figure 8.1 shows the information that must be included.

The school prospectus may well be a parent's first impression of a school. The information it contains will, of necessity, be detailed and will be aimed at a wide catchment of readers. Arguably, the more attractively presented it is and the more professional the nature of the publication, the more it will encourage parents to send their children to the school. O'Connor (1990) gives concise and pertinent advice about optimum methods of compiling the school prospectus. The cost of producing a prestigious publication may be considerable, particularly if colour is used. For school management the challenge is to present the required material within budgetary constraints in an attractive and reader-friendly way, while ensuring that the statutory information is included.

Figure 8.1 Prospectus information – the minimum requirements

- Name, address and telephone number of the school; names of the headteacher and chairperson of governors;
- description of the type of school: for example, county, high, mixed;
- arrangements for visiting the school;
- statement of the curriculum aims of the governing body;
- sex education provided (where it is offered);
- hours in the week spent on teaching;
- dates of the terms and half-terms for the school year;
- a summary of the content of the curriculum for each year group and how it is organized;
- a list of the external qualifications offered, including the names of the syllabuses associated with these qualifications;
- details of any careers education provided and arrangements for work experience;
- the school's religious affiliations, if any;
- particulars of the religious education provided, including information about parents' rights to withdraw their child from RE and collective worship;
- information about how to make a complaint about the delivery of the National Curriculum;
- information about availability in school of documents and regulations related to the National Curriculum;
- details of the school's arrangements for meeting special educational needs;
- particulars about the arrangement for pastoral care and school policy on discipline and uniform;
- particulars of the organization of education in the school;
- for schools in Wales, information about the teaching of the Welsh language;
- information about any extra-curricular activities;
- school session times;
- summary of the governors' charging and remissions policy;
- school policy for external examination entry.

Until such time as the school prospectus is revised it is the duty of the governing body to inform parents of the required information through their annual meeting with them. When revision is under-taken, all statutory information must be contained in one booklet. While legislation places the responsibility firmly at the door of governors, in reality the task of compiling the new-style prospectus will fall on the headteacher and senior staff. If they view its production as an additional burden to their role, they will consider it a chore rather than a valuable communication medium. Equally, if production is delegated to a member of staff with expertise in desktop publishing, who will produce a fine end-product in terms of lay-out, control mechanisms may need to be built into the process. These include regular reviews of the work at various stages, checks on the accuracy of information, checks on whether the information has been correctly and honestly presented and, most important, proofreading by a fairly wide audience, including parents. The prospectus is aimed at convincing them to select the school, which is a particular challenge when those responsible for compilation may have little or no training in persuasive presen-tation, even to fellow professionals.

The process will take time and careful planning. Schools are competing for pupils and therefore the prospectus is more impor-tant now than ever before. Schools need to conduct their own market research to help them identify their strengths and weak-nesses, rather than basing judgements on hunch and subjectivity.

Once produced, the school must consider the value of the pros-pectus. The following critical questions may prove useful in assess-ing its effectiveness (O'Connor 1990):

1 is it comprehensible?
2 is it presentable?
3 will people read it?

Devlin and Knight (1990) consider these issues in greater depth.

Other publications

In addition to the prospectus there are other types of information that must be made available by the school. These include:

1 any HMI reports that refer specifically to the school;
2 schemes of work currently used in the school;
3 syllabuses followed;

4 statutory instruments, including statutory orders for National Curriculum subjects; and

5 a full copy of the arrangements for the consideration of complaints about the school curriculum.

One may be forgiven for asking just how many parents are going to require such information. However, such information may well open up a dialogue between a school and some of its other clients, such as those in industry or further and higher education. Whatever the readership, the implications for schools in their links with parents are the same in this as in other aspects of recent legislation – openness, accountability and responsiveness to client groups.

PARENTS AND SCHOOLS – ENHANCING THE LINKS

Despite the emphasis placed on parental involvement throughout the 1980s and the increased representation of parents on governing bodies, the degree of their influence is as yet largely unknown, other than in cases of opting for grant-maintained status when, by a simple ballot, parents may fundamentally change the future direction of a school. In such specific cases parental influence is definite, undisputed and measurable. In other circumstances the 'new partnership' seems to be having less direct effect.

There exist organizations that have developed mainly to keep parents and governors informed about state education, such as the Advisory Centre for Education (ACE) and the National Confederation of Parent–Teacher Associations (NCPTA). In Wales and Scotland, the Parent–Teacher Associations of Wales (PTAW) and the Scottish Parent–Teacher Council (SPTC) exist. Other bodies involving parents include the Campaign for the Advancement of State Education (CASE) and the National Association for Primary Education (NAPE).

At local level, most British schools have some kind of voluntary organization involving parents. However, in many schools their role has so far been largely one of fund-raising and organizing social events. Indeed, the very existence of a PTA may well be used by headteachers 'to give a false impression of parental involvement in a school' (MacBeth 1989). Johnson and Ransom (1983) refer to the 'uncertainties of aim and scope' of PTAs. Similar uncertainties seem to exist today among parent governors. Parent governors are the sole lay voice among professionals and may consider themselves inferior as a result. Sallis (1988) supports the view that parent governors are unsure of their role, even to the extent of questioning whether they have the same powers as other governors.

Parent governors are not elected specifically to represent the views of other parents, yet there is a strong case for clarification and extension of their role, for four reasons. First, in the future schools will need to liaise far more closely with parents than they have before. Second, the legislative framework now exists whereby parents have greater representation on governing bodies than before and it may be appropriate to raise their status. Third, with training, parent governors could provide useful support in tasks that school management teams could reasonably delegate, for example, the review of the prospectus or consultation with parents on some of the issues raised in this chapter and others. Fourth, parent governors need ownership if they are to develop as useful helpers. They are there to provide a parental perspective and, as such, have a vitally important role to play in many aspects of the development of a school.

Governing bodies currently seem to have evolved the following sub-committee structure: fabric and maintenance; finance; and curriculum. An extended structure (Figure 8.2) might enhance liaison with parents and draw together the specialist areas of governors' work.

The parents' liaison sub-committee might consist of three parent governors, one governor from each of the other sub-committees and a senior member of staff. The aims of such a group should be to keep parents informed of major changes affecting their children and to convene regular, informal meetings with parents.

The agenda would, of course, be dictated by the priorities of the school, but could be extended to include areas of interest to parents. Any of the following might be included:

1 new methods of reporting to parents;
2 homework – how parents can help;
3 small building works – future plans;
4 the national record of achievement;
5 starting secondary school or employment and continuing education;
6 SATs and your child;
7 lettings;

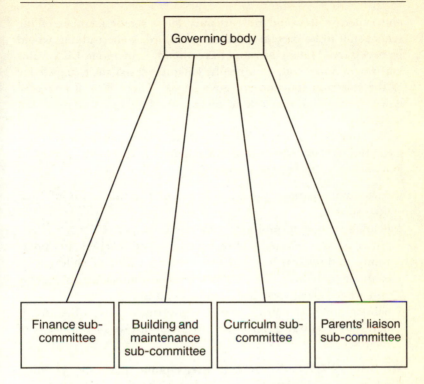

Figure 8.2 An extended structure for a governing body, incorporating a parents' liaison sub-committee

8 the implications of technology in the National Curriculum;
9 the Children Act and its implications;
10 performance indicators; and
11 local management – strengths, weaknesses, opportunities and threats.

The proposal of a new and major role for parent governors presents serious questions, which school managers will have to address. First, and perhaps most fundamental, is the question of how parent governors might take on such a role. Commitment to the need for constructive liaison is a prerequisite for successful partnership. Second, it would also be necessary for parent governors to develop a broad knowledge of the functions of the school and how these functions may be developed within the legal context. Until such time as parent governors themselves possess sufficient knowledge and expertise it would be necessary for a senior member of the school staff to be present at meetings. Third, some training would be necessary. Many governors have already undergone LEA training programmes and, as a result, have increased their knowledge of the role and functions of governance. There is a strong case now for extending that role to include the function of liaison with parents.

Naybour (1989) puts forward a strong case for parental involvement through the model of a home–school association. The main functions of a home–school association are described as:

1 encouraging parents and teachers to talk together in an informal atmosphere;
2 helping schools to project a welcoming image;
3 giving parents, elected parent governors and teachers an opportunity to discuss issues that affect the education of children;
4 enabling parents to understand what is happening in schools and what current teaching trends are; and
5 helping parents to ensure that the governing body, LEA and, if necessary, central government are made aware of the needs of their school.

MacBeth (1989) advocates a twelve-point plan for parental involvement as a minimum programme. The plan includes:

1 a welcoming system;
2 a twice-yearly written report or profile;
3 twice-yearly consultation;
4 a termly class meeting;
5 a parents' association for the school, with class units;
6 a governing body, or, in Scotland, a school board, which makes parents and teachers aware of their educational obligations;
7 publications by the school, to keep parents informed, prepared in consultation with the parents' association;
8 the right of parents to see at any reasonable time all official records on their child;
9 education according to parental wishes – that is, not only should parents be consulted over the main internal decisions affecting their child, but in the case of disagreement every effort should be made to accommodate parental wishes;
10 a system of home visiting, in exceptional circumstances;

11 the constant reiteration by teachers that they provide both a service and a partnership; and

12 teachers making clear to parents that they operate within the constraints laid down by national and local government.

Schools may have the will to set in place such a programme, but it is extremely doubtful that school staff will have the energy or be able to find the resources to set in place such an ambitious agenda of liaison. It is, therefore, all the more relevant for schools to exploit to the full the existing legislative framework in their attempts to increase parental liaison.

CONCLUSION

The method by which school managers will embrace liaison with parents will largely depend on the management style of the head-teacher. The Education Reform Act 1988 opened up a new partner-ship between headteacher and governors, and it is this relationship that should form the basis of enhanced liaison with parents. The machinery is in place, but is the result all that it could be? Liaison with parents will continue on the level at which it has operated hitherto unless school management teams are willing to recognize the need for an enhanced partnership between school and parents. Mechanisms for increasing liaison could be delegated to parent governors, with the support and active involvement of headteacher and staff. Such delegation would not negate the professional–parent partnership, but would enhance the tripartite relationship of school, parents and governors while at the same time giving parent governors shared ownership of the organization they serve. Some school-based training would be necessary, in conjunction with the usual methods of governor training. The increase of parent governor representation can provide the possibility of real, practical help to the headteacher and staff.

Recently, a parent governor spent a morning at the back of my classroom. I believe she enjoyed the activities and I was pleased to have her interest. At the end of the morning she asked me: 'What can I really do to help?' Parent governors want to help. It is appropriate now for school managers to invest in this avenue of support as a means of increasing liaison with the wider parent group.

Chapter 9

Liaising with the media

Peter Reader

Media relations are an increasingly important part of a school's external relations activity. This is in part because there is a growing interest in education generally, but also because educational policy is focusing more attention on the rights of parents both to be informed and to choose. Use of the media is one way of achieving regular and free publicity for a school. This can be an attempt to raise awareness of the school and to create a positive image of the school, but other, more explicit, targets can be set.

One vital part of media relations activity is to communicate with the local community. This community includes the parents of the children at the school. All parents like to be told that their children's school is the best; what better than the endorsement of the school by a third party, the media? The local community also includes prospective parents who may receive little information until near the time when they will have to select a school for their children. Everyone has a fear of the unknown; a school that is known to be active and has a perceived history of 'good news' has an immediate advantage over one that is silent and has a limited external image. The media can also be utilized to enhance the reputation of the school in a number of different ways and indirectly to influence decision-makers: important allies and, potentially, financial friends.

There is another important side of media relations. Little can be done to prevent bad news from getting into the media, but if bad news is seen against a background of a succession of positive reports about the school the damage caused may be limited. The Institute of Public Relations' definition of public relations refers to a planned and sustained effort to maintain goodwill and mutual understanding between an organization and its publics. Successful media relations are critically dependent upon effort and continuity.

How should a school set about tackling media relations? A school that wishes to get a message over to a mass audience has four options: newspapers, magazines, radio and television. Schools are interested mainly in the local audience and magazines are therefore usually an inappropriate medium. There is also the choice between buying advertising space and seeking editorial publicity. While the first costs money, there is no charge for editorial publicity, which is independent of advertising but reaches the same number of people as the advertising. It is also more convincing because readers accept it as factual and unbiased.

Editorial publicity cannot, of course, be guaranteed. Even the best stories about important events in the school's life can seem insignificant to the news editor if there is a more newsworthy story. However, each editor decides independently whether or not to include an item and there are daily examples of stories that fail to make one paper being featured in another. To succeed, it is necessary to try to improve the chances of a story being chosen.

HOW THE MEDIA WORKS

A newsdesk gets information from a large number of sources. Although newsdesks vary in size, the organization is basically the same. Sources include: stories that have been initiated by the journalists themselves; those that have been sent in by news agencies; those that have arrived by post or by fax as press releases; those that have been used elsewhere; and 'tip-offs'. The latter two sources can be used particularly well by schools. In particular, many stories in the regional and local media hinge on the local angle on a national story. For instance, whenever a new document appears about the National Curriculum, regional and local journalists will be seeking opinion from within their area on it. The opportunity to comment as an expert on a national story should not be missed, because, by implication, the school becomes part of the national story, and thus important to the reader, listener or viewer.

It is important to recognize that different sections of the media work in different ways. For schools there are four key areas of the local and regional media to consider: weekly newspapers, whether paid for or free sheets; daily newspapers, particularly evening papers; radio – BBC, independent commercial radio and the newer community stations; and television – BBC and ITV.

Each needs to be handled differently. At one extreme, some weekly newspapers carry few editorial staff and are very dependent on outside contributions to fill their pages; at the other, some news editors receive reams of press releases daily. Clearly, to attract the attention of the hard-pressed news editor, a story must be newsworthy.

Understanding what the media wants is very important. Papers and magazines are bought for their editorial content. Viewers switch on the television or radio because of the editorial content. Editors want to keep and increase their audience, so they will include material that interests that audience. A story needs to be interesting and sent to the right people.

It is helpful to learn how the media works in the local area. No one likes yesterday's news. For many schools, the weekly newspaper is the key medium – and weekly newspapers have deadlines as critical as the most pressured national television newsroom. Try to find out what the deadlines are for local newspapers – for the inside news pages as well as for the front page. Remember that a story that is considered for the front page one week but 'spiked' is unlikely to warrant even a paragraph the next week. Planning is important and alerting a weekly newspaper to a story in advance can pay rich dividends.

Often more than one edition of a newspaper is produced; getting a story into the evening edition of the newspaper for the local area can mean having to provide the journalist with the story very early in the day. Of course, many school stories are not time critical, but it is essential to know in advance what the deadlines are for that all-important story for which there is no advance warning. The key point is that the story must be of interest to the particular audience. Even if it is an exceptionally interesting story, if it is of no relevance to the particular audience it will not be used.

Establishing contacts is also important. All journalists need reliable sources of information. They will trust you if they get to know you and can rely on you. A starting point is to telephone newsdesks in the area and ask for their advice about the best way of giving them information. It helps to have a few good stories in mind when you do this. Being known and trusted for giving accurate information is vital in a crisis. Find out who the education correspondent is; even if there is no formal appointment of an education correspondent, there may be journalists who take a particular interest in education and in schools.

Be prepared to invite local journalists into the school, for social occasions as well. Invitations may not always be accepted, but every time that an invitation lands on a journalist's desk, it reminds him or her that your school exists. Once journalists get to know a contact, they are likely to liaise directly when there is a relevant story. If it is bad news, the school is alerted immediately; if it is good news, it can be capitalized on.

EFFECTIVE MEDIA RELATIONS

Success does not necessarily come overnight. It is important to persevere and to learn from failures as well as successes. Failures often show up a weakness in understanding how the media works. Note who is getting publicity in the local area and try to work out why. If there is no obvious reason, it is probably because they have a better understanding of the way the media works.

It is also important to understand what makes news. Many schools invite the press to the important events in the school calendar, such as prize giving and certificate evenings, but these can be very formal and rather dull occasions. Fun events that provide opportunities for smiling faces in photographs should not be ignored: charity and sponsored events; fund-raising stunts; and, of course, sporting events. Picture editors are always looking for visually exciting shots to brighten up the pages. Other good stories are reviews of concerts and plays, visits by children, work in the community and visitors to the school. Do not forget stories about curriculum developments, and about opportunities for parents and visitors to visit the school. Sending a copy of the school newsletter to the media is often an inexpensive way of gaining publicity, especially in a weekly newspaper.

Clearly, the less local the media, the less chance there is of a story being covered, and it is not sensible to bombard a newsdesk with information that will never be used. Local radio, particularly commercial radio, covers relatively few stories compared with a newspaper.

One of the most effective routes into the newsdesk is provided by the staff journalist, particularly if the school contact has established credibility and courted the interest of the journalist. This route can be used to advantage by suggesting stories that can be given a local angle.

Dealing correctly with journalists is vital. They are busy people and much prefer contacts to be brief and to the point. Being brief also has the advantage that you are less likely to say something that you did not intend. Journalists demand accuracy and honesty, however, and their loyalty is to their audience, not to the contact. In particular, they need answers immediately, not when the contact is ready.

Another factor in being effective is the organization within the school. Some schools are appointing 'press officers' from within the staff. As building up relationships with journalists depends on one-to-one contact this is a desirable development, but who should the press officer be? Headteachers may be too busy and although they will be very active in external affairs for the school, media relations is one area that can safely be delegated – to the right person. The best person is likely to be a full-time member of the teaching staff who already carries some responsibility within the school. It is also important that the press officer is an effective communicator, both in writing and orally, as well as being able to react appropriately should bad news break. Above all, the press officer must be readily contactable, including at home.

For all but the local weekly papers, probably the least effective route into the newsdesk is the press release. However, press releases are a cheap and convenient way of sending the same story to a number of newsdesks and the wordprocessor makes it relatively easy to tailor them to the needs of a particular editor and, hence, to make them more effective. Editors receive dozens of releases each day; it is important to improve the chances of success by following a number of guidelines.

1   Tell the story 'from the top'. This is the most important rule of all. Gimmicky headlines are not necessary – that can be left to the sub-editor – but a suggestion for a headline that sums up the story can be helpful.

2   Tell the story in the first paragraph. Many press releases are skim-read, so do not hide the story. News stories must make an immediate impact on the reader. The first paragraph is usually a concise summary of the entire report, with subsequent paragraphs

adding detail and extending the story. This technique is sometimes referred to as the 'inverted pyramid' approach.

3   Be specific and accurate. Try to answer the following questions: who? what? where? when? why? and how? If the press release does not do this, the journalist will want to, and the very fact that the questions are unanswered may mean that the story is immediately of less interest to the journalist. Be accurate and make sure that names, including first names, addresses and dates are correct.

In particular, pay attention to the following points:

1 clearly identify the origin of the press release;
2 include a contact name and telephone number, including a home number if possible;
3 always indicate the date of the release;
4 include facts, not supposition or opinion;
5 make points clearly, using simple language and short sentences; and
6 avoid educational jargon and acronyms.

4   Use notes to editors. There are many experienced journalists who will argue that you can tell a story in four paragraphs, but with such brevity some of the story can be lost. To avoid this, and to give some background information, use notes to editors. They can also be used for inviting journalists to events.

5   Use quotes. An attributed quote should be included if it adds something to the story. The quote is a chance to express an opinion, which should come from a 'responsible' source, preferably the headteacher or the Chair of Governors. The press officer may well draft these quotes. This will ensure that they are consistent, not only from one week to another, but also in terms of school policy.

6   Provide photographs. Suggesting possible photographs or identifying opportunities for a photo session improve the chances of a story being used. A good photograph is likely to be glanced at by most people who read a journal and this may attract them to read the news item.

INTERVIEWS

Some people dislike being interviewed and stories abound of even experienced professional press officers being 'stitched up' by the media. However, this may have arisen from evasiveness on the part of the interviewee. Many interviews are conducted over the telephone and may not appear to be interviews as such. Journalists will often telephone to check facts that are already in a press release. Often they will be looking for a different quote, one which they think is of more human interest. The contact's tone of voice will be very important: being over-friendly and gushing will quickly signal to the journalist that all is not as it seems, as will reticence and an unwillingness to be helpful. Interviews in person will give the journalist more clues as to whether the contact is 'playing it straight'. Information that is not available or the absence of anyone with first-hand knowledge of the story may be major problems.

Not all interviews are hostile by any means and most will be conducted in a friendly and co-operative way. In a person-to-person interview, background papers about the subject can be discussed with and shown to the journalist, and it makes good sense to have documents already copied for the journalist to take away. Any documents that can only be shown in part to the journalist should not be shown at all.

Radio and television interviews, particularly for the first time, can be stressful. For radio interviews, it is important to talk naturally to the interviewer and maintain eye contact throughout. The interviewer will often signal by a nod of the head if all is going well or when more explanation is needed. Particularly for local news bulletins, many radio interviews are pre-recorded, sometimes over the telephone. The journalist should be asked to replay the tape and almost all will do so; after all, they want the correct story too. Television interviews, particularly in a studio, can seem very contrived but an interview is basically no more than a conversation.

With schools becoming more involved in media relations, interview technique courses are available – at a price. It is worth remembering that most people who are interviewed on television have had no media training, whereas most teachers have had training in presentational skills. One technique often employed is to decide in advance the three key messages that you want to get over and to work them into the answers regardless of the questions.

Two other matters should also be borne in mind. First, consider whether you may need to go 'off the record' at any point. If so, it should be made clear to the journalist at the outset whether or not the information can be made public. Once the journalist has the information it is too late: it is already public knowledge.

Second, with a big story, such as a major project that is about to be launched or a major award to the school, pre-briefing and phased release of the news should be considered. To maximize impact, the story should appear in as many media as possible at the same time. Commonly, a school will start with the local newspaper, and the local evening paper should carry the story on the same day as it appears in the weekly. Radio and television, if appropriate, can be mailed or faxed so that the information gets to them on the same day that it appears in print.

DEALING WITH BAD NEWS

There can be times when the media is 'hostile' and it is necessary to deal with 'disaster limitation', even when the disaster is not of your own making. The best way of limiting problems is to have established relationships with the media already in place and active. If the media know from experience that they can trust the school contact, they will be more amenable to his or her views. This is of particular help in 'protecting' the school, but no matter how good press relations are, it is advisable never to go 'off the record' when disaster strikes.

There are six points that are always worth remembering in this context.

1 Always assume the worst. Plan for the worst situation and things can only get better. In any crisis, determine as quickly as possible who is going to deal with the media, who will speak for the school, who will speak for the governors and how these people can be contacted urgently.

2 Act quickly and take responsibility. Even if there is little information, one of the most positive things to do is to tell people that action is being taken. The media monitor the emergency services hourly or more frequently; be prepared to say something in

response to the first press call. Tell the media what is being done to deal with the emergency. The first intimation of an emergency may come to parents through the media. Although, obviously, they will be concerned, they will be reassured by a report that the school is doing something.

3   Enlist everyone who has a contribution to make. While only one person should speak for the school, there are tasks that can be delegated to others. It is vital, however, not to have people around who do not fully know what is going on and who may unwittingly say the wrong thing to the media.

4   Tell the whole story as accurately as possible. 'No comment' is often taken as an admission of responsibility. Keep to the facts, never add comments and remember confidentiality. Do not give names or addresses of those involved.

5   Maintain an authoritative source of information for as long as necessary. Ensure that the press officer is kept up to date with what is going on and knows everything that is likely to be apparent to a diligent journalist. Dealing with the media can keep one person busy all the time, but he or she must be kept updated. To be authoritative, there must be continuity.

6   Do not be tempted to try any publicity gimmicks to divert attention from the disaster. These inevitably backfire and can trivialize a serious situation. However, if there is another good story from the school there is no need to hold it back. Indeed, in a disaster the press officer will build up a new set of contacts and once the worst is over and journalists become bored with the initial story, something fresh and positive can be attractive.

CONCLUSION

Media relations are an essential component of a school's external relations programme and need to be included in an overall external relations plan. Some resources, particularly time for a press officer, are essential for an effective programme of activity while some forward planning can radically diminish the impact of apparent disasters. Effective media relations can contribute to recruitment of pupils and staff, and may be a useful component in building

up a shared sense of institutional identity. Fear has often characterized the relationship between schools and the media, but a sound
liaison is mutually beneficial.

Chapter 10

Links with industry and employers

Patrick Fullick

The vision for the partnership between education and business is that the two cultures, for too long kept apart, can work together to improve each other's performance and, thereby, raise everyone's standard and quality of life.

The fundamental driving forces behind the developing partnership are the need for mutual respect backed up by each wanting to influence the other. This influence may seem to be chiefly business on education regarding the preparation of a quality workforce, enhanced by education's own desire to enrich learning by exposure to the external world. However, it is increasingly also the other way round on issues concerning the contribution to the quality of life by the business sector.

The key to the success of this process is that in order to gain the respect of the other, each will have to concede the influence the other is seeking.

(Marsden 1991:1)

HISTORICAL PERSPECTIVE

Today, more than ever before, schools are under pressure to look outwards, towards the community in which they exist. In no area is this pressure more acute than in the area of links with industry and commerce. It might be thought that this pressure is born of recent initiatives and legislation, such as the TVEI and the Education Reform Act, but the need to educate the young people of the country in matters pertaining to industry dates back well into the last century.

The first individual to identify and articulate the shortcomings of the British system of education in respect of the nation's industrial needs is generally held to be Sir Lyon Playfair. In his introductory address at the opening of the Government School of Mines in 1851, Playfair pointed out that

> as surely as darkness follows the setting of the sun, so surely will England recede as a Manufacturing nation, unless her industrial population become much more conversant with science than they are now.
>
> (Playfair 1855:1)

The Bryce Commission of 1895 took up the cause for a coherent system of education incorporating science and technical subjects:

> No definition of technical instruction is possible that does not bring it under the head of Secondary Education, nor can Secondary Education be so defined as absolutely to exclude from it the idea of technical instruction.
>
> The system which we desire to see introduced may rather be described as coherences, an organic relation between different authorities and different kinds of schools which will enable each to work with due regard to work done by others.
>
> (Bryce Report 1895:135, 326)

The arguments that had their genesis in the latter part of the nineteenth century eventually found some expression in the Education Act 1944. The Act set out a system of education that subsequent Ministry of Education guidance spelled out as a three-tier system of grammar, technical and modern schools. The technical schools were chosen to concentrate on an education for less academic pupils, 'selecting the sphere of industry or commerce' as an area of preparation for their pupils (Ministry of Education 1947). The Crowther Report (1959) reinforced the vision of technical education as a path for pupils who were not attracted to the academic curriculum of the grammar schools, but this vision became less and less possible to achieve in the next decade as the spread of comprehensive education took a hold throughout the country.

In 1976, in what became called 'the Great Debate', Prime Minister James Callaghan argued that schools were to blame for Britain's poor economic performance, and that contact between schools and industry was insufficient. The need for educational reform was also propounded by Barnett, who, three years later, wrote: 'Education for capability alone can keep

Britain an advanced technological society and save her from being a Portugal, perhaps even an Egypt, of tomorrow' (Barnett 1979:127). The end of the 1970s brought a change in government, with the election of a Conservative administration committed to leading Britain into an industrial and economic renaissance. Although education was not high on the agenda for the new government, the need for industry to take a leading role in educating the nation's young was. The Technical Vocational Education Initiative (TVEI) was launched by the Prime Minister, Margaret Thatcher, on 12 November 1982 in a speech to the House of Commons.

One of the most radical aspects of this initiative was that the Manpower Services Commission (MSC) rather than the DES was given the responsibility for it. LEAs were invited to submit bids for a pilot scheme that would provide pre-vocational education to a group of pupils, incorporating a large degree of industrial and economic awareness. As the initiative was extended to a larger number of schools throughout the middle of the decade, the rather narrow vocationalism of its early days became transformed into a broader vision of education, more characteristic of that envisaged by the Bryce Commission of some ninety years before.

The Education Reform Act 1988, legislating for a National Curriculum in England and Wales, has continued the impetus for curricular change, and it is fairly clear that the TVEI extension policy has become a vehicle for National Curriculum implementation. Incorporating as it does a requirement for the teaching of economic and industrial understanding as one of its cross-curricular themes, the National Curriculum reinforces the ideals of the TVEI extension and acts as a powerful force for the forging of links between schools and industry. The challenge for the 1990s is to forge these links and to make them work.

FORGING LINKS

The initiatives of the 1980s, together with the introduction of a National Curriculum that embraces the notion of industrial and economic awareness, have made it imperative that schools begin to address in earnest the issues involved in making links with industry. The National Curriculum Council provides some compelling arguments:

Throughout their lives pupils will face economic decisions. They will face choices about how they contribute to the economy through their work. They will decide how to organise their finances and which goods and services to spend money on. They will form views on public issues, such as the environmental effect of economic development or the economic arguments involved in elections.

Education for economic and industrial understanding aims to help pupils make these decisions. It explores economic aspects of their present lives. It prepares them for future economic roles: as producers, consumers and citizens in a democracy.

Pupils need education for economic and industrial understanding to help them to contribute to an industrialised, highly technological society. With increasing economic competitiveness, both in the European Community and worldwide, the nation's prosperity depends more than ever on the knowledge, understanding and skills of young people. To meet this challenge pupils need to understand enterprise and wealth creation and develop entrepreneurial skills.

(National Curriculum Council 1990b:1)

Yet schools must consider more than their requirement in law if they are to develop a relationship with industry that is truly beneficial to both sides, and that will do more than provide a brief spell of contact between the two cultures. Indeed, it is likely that poorly planned contact will do little to enhance relationships and may very well be harmful. Teachers may have made a deliberate decision not to work in industry, or may have done so and rejected it. Those in industry may have a partially informed view of education based on media images, their own school-days and parents' evenings at their children's schools. Such poorly formed ideas on both sides are unlikely to be developed by a brief acquaintance in which a speaker from industry comes into a school to talk to a class that he or she perceives as unprepared and unresponsive, while the teacher perceives the speaker as addressing the class at a level that is inappropriate and with language that is far too technical.

It is helpful at this point to consider very briefly what exactly we mean by industry, as the word has many shades of meaning and conjures up for some an image of dark, satanic mills that seems to have little relevance to pupils in a rural first school. The RSA's Industry Year publicity leaflet made a useful statement:

> Industry – the provision of products and services which people need and want – is fundamental to almost everything we do.
>
> (Royal Society of Arts 1986)

This statement provides a definition of industry that includes almost all aspects of life in any local community. It embraces not just the coal mine and the steel works, but also the butcher, the baker and the candlestick maker – and encompasses, too, those areas of the community that we perhaps do not traditionally consider as industrial, such as shops, offices and even hospitals. This is important, for those working in schools need to recognize that industry in this broad sense surrounds any school in any community.

What benefits for education, and more particularly for the individual school, may come out of contact with industry? Rather than answer this question directly, it is helpful to ask what is possible in developing closer contacts between industry and education. This different question has the benefit of also considering what industry has to gain – something that many teachers are very cautious about! Experience shows that the possibilities for working with industry are many and varied. The list given in Figure 10.1 is by no means exhaustive.

Figure 10.1   The possibilities for working with industry

*industrialists in the classroom	*work experience for pupils (an important element for TVEI projects in the secondary phase)
*industrialists as governors	*teacher placements in
*industrialist placements in schools	industry
	*work shadowing (on both sides)
*compacts	*mini-enterprise schemes
*enhancement of the curriculum	*resources from industry
*problem-solving exercises	*industry days
*interview practice	

Teachers are often suspicious of industry's motives for wishing to work with schools, feeling that the prime reason is for industry to market its products. It is, of course, impossible to exclude this motive from consideration – after all, industry exists in order to make and sell, and to ignore the desire of a company to become known to young people is to ignore its whole *raison d'être*. But industry also operates with the consent of the community it serves; those involved in industry generally recognize this and are keen to ensure that informed consent continues to be given. To be sure, there are some examples of blatant company propaganda that have been sent to schools, but thankfully these are relatively few and far between. It is doubtful if many teachers use the same stringent criteria that they apply to the vetting of industrially produced curriculum materials to the vetting of materials received from, say, environmental pressure groups. Yet the worst that most industries can be accused of is enlightened self-interest, wishing to draw attention to themselves and at the same time to contribute to the development of young people and the education system itself through contact with schools.

ACTION PLAN

Assuming that a school decides to establish closer links with industry, how should it proceed? While all schools are different and find themselves in widely differing industrial environments, it is possible to set out a basic plan around which an institution can base its initiative. This action plan is shown in Figure 10.2. The notes that follow explain the steps of the plan and the critical events that need to be made to happen in order to proceed to the next step.

Examine the environment

This step is concerned with establishing the operating environment of the school, and the receptiveness of the institution as a whole to the idea of working with industry. The way in which this examination is carried out will greatly depend upon the quarter from which the initiative comes. What is clear, however, is that any initiative must gain the support of the senior management team of a school and that of the governing body if it is to stand a chance of succeeding. This does not mean that the support must

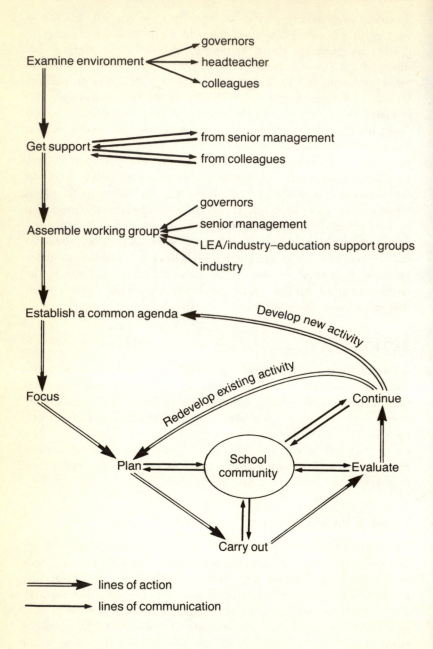

Figure 10.2 Action Plan

be there from the outset – it may well have to be gained – but it does mean that there must be a willingness on the part of those charged with managing the school to support proposed developments, both in terms of broad policy and in terms of allowing the resources for development to take place. If the initiative comes from the headteacher or from the senior team of the school, this stage may be reasonably straightforward, otherwise support must be gained by the staff member or members whose idea it is.

Exceptionally, an initiative of this sort may come from outside the school. It will be particularly important in this case to manage such an initiative carefully so that the school retains ownership of what it sees as its area of responsibility – the curriculum – while still allowing progress. Lines of communication will also be significant here. External initiators will need to ensure that they have cleared the correct channels in the school before proceeding to have discussions directly with members of the teaching staff of the school.

In certain circumstances, care may be needed before seeking the support of the governing body. If there has been no history of school–industry links, despite the presence of people from industry on the governing body, it is very likely that no need for this has been perceived by those on the governing body or by the senior staff of the school. While this does not, in itself, mean that the willingness to develop links cannot be established, it does mean that in seeking support for links implicit criticism must be avoided at all costs, otherwise support is most unlikely to emerge.

Get support

Having determined that the school environment is one in which the discussion of school–industry links is likely to be productive, gaining the support of those charged with managing the school is vital in these early stages. Successful links with industry will certainly involve curricular change of some sort or another. If they do not, the effect will be marginal at best, as the changes will not have become assimilated into the school's structure. Such changes may be principally in terms of timetable – the setting up of a 'problem-solving with industry day', for example – or they may involve longer-term developments in the school's programmes of study – the introduction of aspects of industrial and economic awareness into certain areas of the school, for example.

Whatever change occurs, it can only occur with the support of the staff. Informal discussion may be needed, and may be very effective. A paper presented to the routine staff meeting may be useful to appraise staff of the possibilities. Heads of departments will be keen to know the implications for their subject areas. Those charged with the pastoral care of pupils may ask about any benefits there may be for PSE and careers education.

Those responsible for proposing the initiative should be clear about what they are seeking to do and what benefits their ideas have for the school, and should allow others to influence the possible outcomes. It is at this point that teachers' suspicion of industry and its motives for involvement in education is likely to be most in evidence. Those responsible for proposing the developments will need to be ready for such resistance and ready to counter it.

Support may also be sought at this stage from agencies outside the school which may be helpful in promoting change – a list of these, together with contact addresses, is given in the Appendix on page 220. The aim is to ensure that the initiative proceeds with the consent of colleagues in the school, and that their involvement is at a level that satisfies them – in other words, ownership of the project by the institution and the individuals within it.

Assemble a working group

In order to develop the intention to work with industry into action it will be necessary to get together a group of individuals who are able to take the initiative further. This group should be drawn from a broad constituency and it should involve all those who have a stake in the developing links, including representatives from industry. The size of this group may vary, with five as a likely minimum number and the upper limit determined by the observation that the work accomplished is sometimes inversely proportional to the number of members of a group! Membership along the following lines is suggested:

1 the proposer of the initiative;
2 a representative of the school's teaching staff;
3 a member of the school's senior management team;
4 a member of the governing body;

5 a representative of the LEA or a school–industry support
  agency; and
6 representatives of local industry.

The greatest challenge at the outset is to decide how to approach
representatives from industry to serve on the group. This is not
critical, as it is always possible to find other interested individuals
once the initiative is on the way, and in any case the school–industry support services in the region should be able to help in doing
this. It is easy to invite new individuals to serve on the group,
but it may be very difficult to get those whose contribution is less
than helpful to leave it. The name of the group is a small point
at this stage, but will help those outside it to identify its purpose.
Whatever the name chosen, it should be clear that the team is
responsible for the development of links between the school and
industry – and if the resulting acronym is original and memorable,
so much the better!

Establish a common agenda

The quotation at the beginning of this chapter is especially valuable to bear in mind at this stage of the action plan. If a school
is to develop links with local industry that are profitable and
lasting, it is essential that there is trust between the two sides.
Just as the first stages of the initiative are concerned with the
development of ownership within the school community, this stage
is concerned with the development of a partnership between industry and education. This atmosphere cannot develop without
mutual trust and the assurance that neither side has a hidden
agenda. The way to ensure this, apart from the exhortation to be
open, is to set a joint agenda for action where both sides feel
happy with the aims of what is being proposed and the objectives
that are being set. In addition, effective communication should
ensure that all those who have a stake in the initiative are kept
informed by their representatives. The initial task should be to
begin to explore areas of mutual interest: where those on the
education side feel that there is a need or opportunity for development work, and where those on the industry side feel that they
wish and are able to help in this development. Such exploration
will lead to a number of possible areas for collaboration which
will require closer examination and further development later.

Once the exploratory work is under way and the team is coming together, a policy statement should be developed. This should be simple and broad, as it is intended as a statement of mutual intent, and should commit no one to a particular course of action. If it is too prescriptive it will need frequent amendment, which will do it and those who drew it up no credit at all and will destroy its purpose in guiding the team's future activity. Far better to restrict a policy statement to a set of simple guidelines at this stage and allow it to become more elaborate later on.

Focus

With a simple statement of policy and a set of mutually agreed possibilities for further work together, the team is now in a position to decide where it will focus its attention initially. As in many other areas, linking schools and industry is a process better accomplished at a leisurely pace rather than at a breakneck gallop. Far better to attend to one idea at a time and then turn attention to other matters, having accomplished something reasonably satisfactorily, than to try to do too many things at once.

This step of the plan, therefore, is concerned with deciding what to tackle first. The criteria for making this decision should be:

1 priority – in respect of school, national and LEA policies;
2 resources – what resource implications do the various areas of agreed action have?; and
3 time-span – as a first venture it is likely to prove better to tackle a project that has a fairly short time-span rather than one which requires long-term implementation.

Plan

Having agreed on the initial work, the team must then begin to plan what needs to be done. Smaller working parties may be set up and different members of the team may take roles within these so that each acts as a hub of activity, enabling a set of tasks to be accomplished and co-ordinated, and a programme to be set out.

Implement

The programme for the activity will have assigned roles to individuals inside and outside the school. Whatever the activity, teachers will almost certainly retain control over pupils, even if someone from industry is directly involved. It will be necessary to make sure that all those participating know what is expected of them. The management of the school and its pupils is the responsibility of those on the education side of the partnership. Those on the industry side of the partnership will have undertaken their own responsibilities, too, and should be allowed to fulfil them.

Evaluate

The evaluation of development work is very valuable and is vital in this particular context if the partnership is to be maintained and developed. A date for reviewing the activity should be set in advance of carrying it out. Review meetings should ensure that all those involved in developing the activity have a chance to make a contribution so that it can be reshaped and developed further. In addition, if a substantial contribution has been made to the activity by those from industry it is only right that they should know where they stand and whether the activity has been worth while for the school. The education side of the partnership should be equally keen to establish the value of the activity to those industries involved.

Continue

At this point further development can take place, properly the aim from the outset. This development may take several forms:

1 the activity may be replanned and reshaped as part of the evaluation process, and then run again subsequently;
2 new activities may be developed, identified from the original common agenda established; and
3 the successful joint activity may be disseminated and publicized: to the rest of the school, to parents and governors, and to the local community. A school that, having sought and gained the assent of its partners in industry, publicizes its work in this way will find it easier to attract partners for activities in the future.

GENERAL POINTS ABOUT THE ACTION PLAN

The plan indicates the process of planning and developing links, and emphasizes the sequence that is appropriate, together with the communications that are required. It should be noted that an especially strong emphasis is laid on communications between the team and the rest of the school. Keeping staff informed about developments and inviting comments help to maintain the ownership of the initiative generally among the staff instead of confining it to a small group, with whom it may become identified as some sort of élite development.

At no point in the action plan is mention made of money. Approaching industry for money can work, but if a school intends to do this, it should be direct, honest about it and should not claim that it is part of an attempt to cultivate a long-term relationship. A school should certainly not make approaches for money to any industry with whom an action plan of this sort is being followed. The plan emphasizes the agreement of a mutually disclosed agenda, which cannot be done if one party aims to get something for nothing from the other. Once joint agreement about worthwhile activities is obtained, both parties have an in-built incentive to invest in planning and implementing them, in terms of time and resources.

CASE STUDY

For simplicity, the case study is presented as a single school's experience, although it is in fact compiled from the history of several schools. The school is a secondary school in a southern county of England, with pupils in the age range 11–18. There is no local heavy industry, but there are many companies concerned with electronics and electrical engineering in the area, a number of financial institutions and companies involved with exploration for and production of oil and natural gas. The school's first venture into work with industry was as part of a curriculum project designed to enrich the education of pupils through activities set in a real-life context. This was set up with the help of several local companies. A small group of teachers took part in planning the work, which was carried out with one of four forms of year 9 pupils over a one-year period. The venture did not develop further after this period and contact with the companies ceased.

Subsequently, new staff at the school sought to re-establish links with industry. The active support of the headteacher and the senior management team at the school was obtained, and one member of the team was assigned the responsibility for industrial contact. Representatives of local companies were already members of the governing body of the school, and, together with the senior member of staff responsible, formed the nucleus of a group named the Industrial Liaison Group (ILG), chaired by a member of the governing body of the school who was also a middle manager in a local company. The group's membership came from the teaching staff of the school, industry – with an attempt to reflect the balance of local industry's interests and activity – the school's senior management and the governing body. Staff from organizations involved with local industry–education links were invited to contribute to meetings as the need arose.

The first meetings of the ILG identified some areas of common interest. The ILG discussed these and decided to concentrate on developing a careers/industry education programme throughout the school. One of the companies represented on the ILG had recently undertaken a management audit, and used this experience to devise a curriculum audit of careers/industry topics throughout the school curriculum. The audit was conducted using the head of careers, heads of department, main-scale teachers and pupils. The picture of careers/industry education that emerged as a result of this was one of extreme fragmentation, with each party having widely different perspectives of what formed the curriculum. As a result, a comprehensive programme was devised, with implementation in stages subject to review after each stage was in place.

Analysis

The school's first links with industry were made through a desire to influence curriculum development and resemble the links made by many schools. This initiative did not prove to be long term due to its very limited ownership, as development concerned only a limited number of staff and one form of one year. There was thus very little effect on the overall curriculum. This was exacerbated by the structure of the initiative, which was viewed by the rest of the school staff, and to some extent by those directly involved in it, as a rather élitist activity. Communication of the work to the rest of the staff was also poor, with many staff being unaware of what was happening and heads of department not being informed of the work that was being done in the areas for which they were responsible.

The subsequent attempt at developing links occurred in a more structured way, with recognition of the need for ownership of the project by the whole school. The ILG also recognized at the start the need to draw up a mutual agenda so that each side was aware of the other's aspirations and interests. Through the use of industrial expertise, the ILG established itself as part of the apparatus for change in the school, underpinning the work of the staff at all levels and providing a focus for development work. As a result of the integral incorporation of this initiative into the school's work, the industrial partners perceived the whole development to be of great value to both sides of the partnership and were prepared to provide the resources required for implementation. This initiative shows every sign of continuing in the long term, with partners able to influence the next stage of the process through the integral review procedures.

Chapter 11

The school within the community

John Watts

No school, not even an approved school, is totally isolated from its surrounding community. There is bound to be some correspondence, if only because the school relies on the local infrastructure and its maintenance, with consequent contact between teachers, students, delivery services and other agencies such as police, health departments and the suppliers of services including telecommunications and electricity. On the other hand, the monastic tradition, which runs strongly through the history of education, has resulted in a tendency for the teaching profession to isolate its pupils and institutions as far as possible from the hurly-burly of everyday life. It is not so long ago that the headmaster of any respectable public school would be expected to be in holy orders, and the quasi-religious trappings of maintained schools, including morning assembly, prayers and compulsory religious education, have all added to the other-worldliness of schools.

However much this cloistering of the classroom has been relaxed in recent years, its long-term effects are not easily shaken off. There are still schools whose headteachers forbid parents to pass the main gates without an appointment. There is, of course, a seductive logic to this sort of over-protectiveness, as their staff in many cases thank their headteacher for being relieved of the pressure that would otherwise be inflicted upon them. Ultimately, however, this sustained apartness reinforces the mystique that has surrounded school teaching, with its message to parents that they should stand well back.

Private and boarding schools recruit nationally and internationally, which, paradoxically, increases isolation from the local community at the same time as helping to create broader solidarity between young people from far and wide. The vast majority of schools, however, are neighbourhood schools, drawing upon a catchment area. This holds true even since the introduction of open access under the Education Reform Act 1988. Since the decline of selective schooling, when boys and girls were divided at age eleven between the modern and the grammar schools, it is likely that those born in the same street will attend the same schools as their contemporaries from five to sixteen. Thus a school has a catchment area, ragged at the edges, but carrying an identity.

This identity is primarily geographical; it does not necessarily define a community. Whichever of the five hundred definitions of 'community' we choose, we cannot escape the incorporation of a sense of common interests among its members. There will be a certain sense of common interest among the parents of a given school in that their children will attend it, but this is no guarantee that other interests will coincide. The clientele of any one school may include Catholics and Protestants, Muslims and Seventh Day Adventists, Labour voters and Tories. In other words, there will be a variety of interests represented and these may often be in conflict with one another. On the other hand, those holding these various convictions and intentions will tend to recognize each other, to be for the most part on negotiating terms with each other. One definition of 'community' is that it is a group of people who tell stories about each other, gossip, in the non-malicious sense, being what holds them together. This is a helpful way of perceiving community, in that it does not require that its members are all of one mind or living in perfect harmony with each other, only that they are bound by certain common concerns and expectations. It is this meaning of the word that will be used here to refer to a school's community.

Before considering the management of relations between a school and its community it will be necessary to examine the range and diversity of those relationships. The management of a 'closed' school, one that minimizes the contacts that exist between it and the outside world, will be very different from the management of an 'open' school, one that engages at all possible points with its community, by means that will be detailed a little further on. The management of external relations at a closed school will be confined to a few staff. The headteacher will act as the gatekeeper, seeing parents, whenever possible without disrupting the teaching timetables of the staff, conducting most meetings with officers and outside agencies, such as police and social services, acting as spokesperson to the media and liaising with other schools via their headteachers. There may well be a careers teacher, if the school is secondary, and there will be staff representatives on the governing body and the PTA if there has to be one. But for the most part teachers in the closed school will operate the internal system with minimum reference to individuals and organizations outside the gates. The curriculum may be interchangeable with that of many other closed schools as it has no reference to the history, locality, interests or problems of the surrounding community. In management terms, the headteacher of the closed school is The Manager and need not concern this chapter any further.

It is virtually impossible for a school to develop a broad relationship with its community while retaining a management style appropriate for a closed school. Certain moves in the direction of openness might take place, but these would rapidly affect the internal management or else be at odds with it. For example, the headteacher and staff of a relatively closed primary school might decide to invite parents to morning assembly once a week. In the course of this increased contact between parents and teachers, the concerns or interests of the parents would tend to emerge or to be aired.

The parents, for example, might offer to contribute to the weekly assemblies. Staff would be obliged to respond, one way or another, and there would be pressure on the headteacher to share some of the responsibility for the conduct of internal proceedings. If this is conceded, in a small way a shift of management style will have occurred. Further links with parents or other members of the public may bring other changes or new conflicts in their wake. Most significant changes are incremental in this kind of way: the question is whether the changes occur as a consequence of policy or in spite of the *status quo*, and whether the management style undergoes changes in keeping with the development.

There is no boundary line, therefore, marking off 'a community school' from a 'non-community school', an open school from a closed school. The distinction is a matter of degree. Where change and development have occurred, they could be plotted along a continuum. It may be useful, therefore, to examine the features of a fully fledged community school, to set up a model against which any individual school may be matched for correspondences. The case for openness has been argued elsewhere, and the term community school will now be used to imply maximum openness.

MODELS OF THE COMMUNITY SCHOOL

In order to consider the management of external relationships in a community school, it will be useful first to establish a model of such a school. While the definition of community education and the formulation of its aims have occupied many pages of published and unpublished material, relatively few attempts have been made to delineate the profile of a community school. The most frequently discussed has probably been that offered by Skrimshire (1981). She identified six stages of community schooling in a sequential development:

1 neighbourhood school;
2 school with strong home links;
3 school with community curriculum;
4 dual use;
5 school with community participation and control; and
6 school as agent for community development.

Although it is useful to pinpoint each of these functional conditions in a school's relationship to its community, the model has two major shortcomings. First, it suggests a sequence that hardly corresponds to experience in the ways that a school might develop, and second, it fails to take account of the great diversity of features that may form part of the framework of a community school. There is no evidence to support the implication that a school will progress from one stage to the next in the model and, indeed, the manifestation of a community-based curriculum is the rarest feature of all to be found in schools that have otherwise evolved considerable community links. If there is a place for the community curriculum in a developmental model, it should properly be sited at the end. Developments are almost invariably related to local circumstances, such as a new headteacher or a response to a sudden spate of unemployment among school-leavers, or the enthusiasm of one member of staff. Developments will, therefore, always be peculiar to the particular school.

To meet these criticisms, an alternative model is offered here. Leaving aside the question of developmental sequence, the following might be considered as the identifying features of the idealized community school.

The school as a community

1 The school is a community which embodies reciprocal care between its students and staff, both teaching and non-teaching.
2 Transactions are conducted by negotiation rather than by coercion and confrontation.
3 Management is open and responsibilities are shared.
4 There is both policy and practice relating to equal opportunities, with regard to race, creed, gender and age.

The school's relationship with its community

1 The school is aware of, and responsive to, the concerns, needs and aspirations of its community/ies.
2 The school is familiar with, and uses, the resources for learning within the community.
3 The school introduces all possible contributors from the community into its daily work and learning programmes.
4 The school's resources for learning are accessible to the community.
5 The school offers its social amenities to the community.

Curriculum and studies

1 The community dimension is recognized in all subjects and all levels of the curriculum as an integrating factor.
2 Studies are tailored to individual needs, interests and competences.
3 Studies maintain a balance between individual and group activities.
4 Students are guided to enable them to identify problems, devise strategies for solving them, retrieve information, form and test hypotheses, present their findings, to own what they learn and yet to share it.

Values

1 The school creates a climate in which the personal development of all staff and students is encouraged as a matter of course.
2 The climate is one that expects and assists self-appraisal among all staff and students.

3 The climate is one that creates an expectation of the highest
standards of academic, expressive, practical and social achievement.

In case this seems a tall order, it should be noted that no known
school fits the model on all counts. It may be of interest, however,
for a school to check its practice against the model to see what
its own current profile looks like, and to use the results of such
an audit to help to decide what direction any development might
take. It should be obvious, on the other hand, that many schools
will exhibit some of the sixteen features in the model, without
claiming the full status of a community school. Again, it might be
argued that, ultimately, this is only a model for delivering full and
rounded education to all. This in turn raises the issue of whether
community education is simply 'good' education. It is sufficient to
claim that there is no single determining feature of the community
school, that most schools are community schools to some degree
or other, and that what is really of interest for any given school
is the stage of development it has reached within each of the
aspects of the above model.

HISTORICAL DEVELOPMENT OF COMMUNITY SCHOOLS

There is a sense in which community education may be seen as
the original and universal means by which one generation has
passed on and developed its culture to the next. Before the emergence of teaching as a discrete occupation and the building of
schools, what needed to be learned was gathered by the young
from their elders, families, neighbours and workmates. There is
evidence to show that this is still how we learn most of what we
need to know (Tough 1988). However, the introduction of compulsory schooling and prescribed curricula, along with the adoption
of the clerical tradition of teaching, divorced institutions of education from the everyday life of the community to the point where,
quite heretically, the common belief was that education comprised
only what was learned in school and college.

The best teachers have known instinctively that learning cannot
be separated from living and the normal world of family and
neighbourhood. Such teachers have often suffered for it: their
efforts have often been resisted or derided by the profession and
the establishment, sometimes quite vindictively. The story of

Teddy O'Neill in *The Idiot Teacher* (Holmes 1977), a significant enough title, is illuminating in this respect. But such scattered cases tell how powerful the hold of the academic mystique has been, and it was only when a chief education officer was able to incorporate the ideas of community education into the maintained provision of a local authority that we saw a replacement model coming into existence.

Henry Morris accomplished just this in his years as chief education officer in Cambridgeshire. His plan first appeared in an internal memorandum dated 1925 and represents a landmark in the history of public education. The memorandum is reproduced in full by Rée (1973). Morris presented a vision of education that was to be built around what he called village colleges. The village college was to act as the cultural centre for local life, not only the place for schooling, but the site for adult learning, festivals and recreation. The village college was, no less, to take the place that had long been vacated by the church, around which life had revolved in earlier centuries. He saw the village college

> as the community centre for the neighbourhood, which would provide for the whole man (*sic*), and abolish the duality of education and ordinary life. It would not only be the training ground for the art of living, but the place in which life is lived, the environment of a genuine corporate life.
>
> (Rée 1973)

The extraordinary thing about Morris is that, in the teeth of every conceivable obstacle, at a time when the country was in deep economic depression, he brought this dream to life. By the time Morris retired there were five village colleges in existence and others on the drawing board. At first it was thought that the village college concept might be appropriate for rural districts but had no application in the urban setting. It was not until 1959, nearly thirty years after the opening of the first village college at Sawston, that Lawrence Weston School, the first urban school modelled on Morris's pattern, was opened in Bristol, with Cyril Poster, a former village college teacher, as its headteacher. Since then, the spread of the Morris idea into various forms, rural and urban, has continued right up to the present.

STYLES OF MANAGEMENT

As an administrator, Morris was well aware of the need for the village colleges to have forms of management different from those of the ordinary school with its orthodox board of governors. If the activities of the college were to meet the needs of the community, there had to be closer representation of the local interests. Furthermore, the same degree of attention had to be given to the pursuits of adult users as to those of children in the daily conduct of the college. To achieve the first aim, an elaborate and subsequently top-heavy new form of governing body was created, with every district and parish council in the catchment area represented, and instead of a headteacher, a warden was appointed to be responsible for the combined school and adult centre. As it turned out, the warden was invariably a headteacher drawn from school experience, with an interest in adult education, and never someone recruited from adult or further education. There was an adult tutor, who was responsible to the warden, thus ensuring, as far as possible, that there was co-ordination of the administration, use of premises and planning of events. The governing body had supervision of the financial arrangements of the whole college.

In practice, the provision for adults tended to be quite separate from the school life and curriculum, but the adults had excellent accommodation in their own wing and access to a joint school—county branch library. Only in later years was the criticism levelled that the community provision was 'bolted on'. However true this may have been of certain cut-price versions of the village college, with what came to be termed 'dual-use' of premises, no one who has experienced the long-standing institutions of Sawston and Impington colleges, the first two built before 1939, could describe their adult provision as being a 'bolt-on' afterthought.

The central problem of management for a community school is reconciling the priorities of statutory full-time schooling with those of the community users, whether pre-school or adult. In every local authority that has established such multiple provision, the final decision of priority has rested with the governing body and the headteacher. Unfortunately, the governing body, with representation from the local community to moderate its decisions, has always been appointed primarily to ensure the welfare of the school and its full-time students. This has caused those staff with particular responsibility for community activity in the school, and those chosen to speak for the community and its interests, to feel repeatedly that they are the poor relations and the second-class citizens in the education of the community as a whole. If resources were unlimited, this conflict would not be difficult to resolve. In the world we live in, there are always competing claims on what is available, in terms of cash, accommodation, equipment and staffing.

Various approaches have been made to minimize this problem. In Leicestershire, the earliest local authority to develop a county-wide system of community colleges, a balance was established by the creation at each college of a community council with a constitution engrossed by bye-law. Under this dispensation, a community council was set-up with prescribed representation of the users, of certain other categories, such as young people under eighteen, the school staff and the governors. The council elected its own officers and three representatives on to the governing body. The college principal was, *ipso facto*, a member of the council and the senior community staff member, later to be designated a vice-principal of the college, was its secretary. There is no doubt that the chairperson of a community council was somebody who could have considerable weight in the decision-making of the college, and, where things worked at their best, was a known and familiar person about the premises. It was, however, virtually unknown for a chairperson of council to have any part in curriculum issues in the school. The chairperson would be a governor, but the governing body as a whole had, by its constitution, final overriding authority and would, if necessary, assert it.

The most significant step forward in the Leicestershire provision, as it emerged in the 1960s, was the financial freedom given to the community council. A central tenet of community education is that it promotes the autonomy and empowerment of its participants, which in practice means that they are encouraged to undertake their own planning in identifying community needs and designing the programmes that will meet them. Traditionally, and Morris can be held to account for this in some degree, the providers, as the professionals, have assumed that they know best what the people need and how that can best be catered for. In other words, the provision has been top–down. It is all too easy to fall into the trap of a self-fulfilling prophecy by creating courses and clubs that become well supported and show laudable enrolment figures at a community college, while other needs have never been identified and met. There are always many more people in the community who are not using the facilities than are attending the advertised activities. This results most readily from the professionals being the prime decision-makers. What Leicestershire made possible was a provision that could be decided upon by the representative users, by a system of budget finance, where the professionals were guides but not final arbiters. The only safeguard against a total loss of control, one that would create an impasse between county council and local college users, was the technical power of veto by the principal, the governing body or the director of education. In ten years as a principal in Leicestershire, however, I never recall such power of veto being exercised anywhere in the county.

The budget finance scheme, in essence, enabled a community council to set up classes and clubs, charging fees that were fixed at its discretion. All the local authority required was that at the end of the day the books should balance and a required return of money was made to the county. This enabled the community council of a college to arrange its own priorities and to rob Peter to pay Paul. If, for example, it was felt that a morning crèche was desirable to free young mothers to attend classes, the college community council could subsidize it by lowering the fee and by installing equipment. This was accomplished by maintaining a relatively high fee for well-subscribed groups, such as the badminton club. Although there were inevitable differentials between councils in the different districts of the county, with the market towns enjoying considerable revenue compared to the centres nearer the city of Leicester, the scheme did enable those who planned wisely to accumulate funds for forward planning. Some, indeed, had such heady bank balances at times as to enable them to challenge the authority of the county officers, for example, over such matters as the terms of appointment of tutors. They paid the pipers and could call the tunes. There were crunch times in the county when the national economy faltered, as in 1975, and drastic cuts were threatened in community education. Then community councils united to show the power that they had in asserting their share of the ownership of the colleges. But that is another story.

Other local authorities have created mechanisms for balancing the management of community schools with the provision for local community education. Derbyshire LEA, in 1988, introduced a county-wide structure that placed powers of financial control of community education budgets with councils that were outside the management of the schools and headteachers. Any one council had jurisdiction over the provision that would be made through a group of schools, without identifying with any one of them in particular. This was intended to ensure a fair distribution of resources. A community tutor was appointed to act as the professional guide to each council, while remaining responsible to one particular headteacher as line manager.

This immediately caused a conflict of loyalty and responsibility that put many tutors in impossible positions. They were at one and the same time a member of one school's staff and officer of a supposedly impartial community council. The community tutor, by whatever name, in any local authority scheme, has always run the additional risk of becoming bogged down in administration, to the detriment of field work that would update the assessment of needs and the contacts with local individuals and organizations necessary for meeting them. Wallis and Mee (1983), in their classic study of claims and performance in community schools, found this choking of the community tutor well nigh universal.

Cambridgeshire underwent a reorganization of its provision in 1989 in an effort to break the total control of community provision held by the wardens of the village colleges. The commitment and effectiveness of the various wardens to community education was, not surprisingly, diverse. In the new scheme, the county was divided into thirty patches. Each patch established a community council with responsibility for utilizing the funds allocated by the local authority for community provision in the area. That money was no longer allocated directly to the village colleges. A co-ordinator was appointed to each patch and although in some cases the patch co-ordinator was the local village college warden this was not invariably the case. This put the cat among the pigeons and necessitated a period of intensive negotiation before the scheme, in a much amended form, could become operational.

It is still too early to determine whether the structure of Cambridgeshire's patch administration has avoided the pitfalls of the Derbyshire scheme. What is significant is that these are two large rural LEAs, one claiming to be the cradle of community education, where control of the provision of community education has been shifted from the hands of the schools, where Henry Morris had originally placed it, towards a more democratically constructed body of community representatives. In power terms, this has reduced the nominal strength of the school headteachers and raised the significance attached to grass-root community. However, as always, things are not that simple.

The Education Reform Act 1988 has greatly increased the powers of governing bodies. In the eyes of the Act, a community school is merely one where the premises are, at certain times, used for purposes other than the schooling of those in full-time statutory education. In such cases it is deemed that these uses are the responsibility of the governing body. So, although guidelines may be issued by the local authority as to procedures and charges for public lettings, it is entirely up to governors to decide who shall and who shall not use school premises, and for what purposes, and at what cost. This effectively returns the control of community activity in the school to the headteacher and governors. Plus ça change, plus c'est la même chose? Perhaps it is not quite the same and power will never be as concentrated as in the days of the old school-based community education. In practice, governing bodies will treat with community councils, and the community tutors or patch co-ordinators or whatever they happen to be called locally will steel their nerves and act as go-betweens for the greater good of the users and the protection of their interests. The British tradition is one of checks and balances and, if the balance has shifted, there are new checks to ensure that, even if perfect justice is never established, at least there will be a reasonable degree of fair dealing.

CONCLUSION

For governing bodies and headteachers the greatest managerial problem arises from their responsibility for ensuring that the interests of the school students are paramount. They need to weigh the cost of the use of school facilities by members of the community against the benefits, sometimes intangible, that derive not only from fee revenue, but also from the educational and social advantages of having an adult presence in the school. The fee revenue, if it is not raised to the level of diminishing returns, will seldom meet the cost of wear and tear on plant; on the other hand, there are advantages to students from having a vastly increased range of sources of learning and a sense of the curriculum being more relevant to life as they know it outside the walls.

The balance struck will turn on the convictions held by governors, under the influence of the professionals, parents and community spokespersons. In some schools, the budgets, now controlled by the governing bodies, will be sacrosanct and untouched by appeals from community; in others, some financial return from fees, augmented by funds raised from other local sources, will ensure that certain community needs are met within the school, with the blessing of the governors. Ideally, budgets will be struck after consultations between governors, parents and whatever form of local representative community council has come into existence. The priorities and the emphases will vary from district to district, even when sited close to each other, depending on the strength of the various parties with interests at stake. In one area there may be much activity to support mothers and toddlers, in another it may be the elderly who are given high priority, and so on. This seems to be the outcome of a democratic process and cannot be rendered uniform by standardizing the management provision across a county or borough, let alone the nation. The only feature of management that is likely to be common is the increased degree of shared or corporate responsibility arising from an increased measure of community involvement.

Whatever the scheme of management, however, one thing is certain. Education cannot be, if it ever was, divorced from politics. This does seem to have wider recognition at last, and, as a consequence, teachers, headteachers and other professionals need to develop a political 'nose' if they are to serve their schools and communities or even, nowadays, to remain in business. There is no longer any place for academic ivory towers: a school has to give ear to the interests of the community, in the widest sense of the local population, including its students and their parents, but also its community's employers in commerce and industry, its other public agencies, its voluntary bodies and its political workers. Without such a well-developed 'nose', the headteacher will fail to sense prevailing moods, the sensitivities that must be respected, the needs that might be met and the persons whom it is advisable to court or to avoid. In this, the headteacher cannot stand alone, so that whatever form of management is appropriate at any given school, it is bound to be more open and more attuned to the community. No headteacher may nowadays proclaim, as did the famous Thring of Uppingham School, 'Here I stand supreme, and will brook no interference'. Thring's achievements as an innovator have become part of educational history, but today the leadership that will be followed, and is most likely to find the best advantage for all concerned, will probably be more of a corporate nature and its management will reflect that style.

Part 4

The marketing environment

Chapter 12

Institutional identity in the school context

Nicholas Foskett

All organizations possess an identity and image. The generation of image is an accepted part of the commercial world, and there are few companies that do not set out to cultivate a particular image of themselves. Such images are the product of directed endeavour in the organization and are an integral part of the company's whole existence. For most educationists, however, there is a feeling that image is somehow dishonest, a false creation trying to encapsulate a truth that is, at best, only truth in part and, at worst, a blatant and intentionally misleading lie promulgated to make commercial gain from a naïve and trusting public.

A second consideration, however, may reveal a different perspective. In the headed notepaper that the school or college uses there may well be an institutional identity – a school crest, a Latin motto or the name of the institution in a particular form or typeface. At the school gate there may well be a sign indicating the school name, headteacher and caretaker. Many schools have a school uniform. All are part of the institution's image, created over the years, without overt reference to 'institutional identity programmes', but with clear aims in terms of communicating with external audiences.

Every organization has more than one image. It has the image it would like to project, it has the reality as it is perceived by those who work within it and it has the image that is perceived by those beyond its boundaries. In reality it may have as many images as there are audiences. Further afield, the school will have an image in the wider community at local, county or regional level, and it may well have a national image through its contacts with the media.

Image and institutional identity have always been present in education, from the public schools of the nineteenth century to the comprehensives of today. Many have sought to develop an image in the traditionally acceptable areas of uniform, crest and motto. However, the growth of interest in identity is a phenomenon in the state sector of the last decade and, in particular, the period since the Education Reform Act 1988. This has arisen from the overt move towards competition between schools in terms of recruitment of pupils and staff, and the financial consequences of the process. The independent sector has been aware of the need to cultivate and manipulate image for recruitment benefits throughout its existence, and now the state sector is beginning to consider some of the issues. This suggests that image is all about recruitment. In fundamental terms this may be true, but recruitment is only one of the benefits of an effective programme and, indeed, is itself dependent upon the impact of institutional identity in many spheres.

THE NATURE OF INSTITUTIONAL IDENTITY

Before considering this issue in depth it is appropriate to clarify some of the terminology that is used in this field. The three most common terms in the commercial sector are 'corporate personality', 'corporate identity' and 'visual identity', but negative associations with the word 'corporate' make it more appropriate to modify these in an educational environment to 'institutional personality', 'institutional identity' and 'visual identity'. Let us consider what each means.

Institutional personality

This is the reality of what an institution is, how it operates, what its internal and external relationships are like, and what its actual goals and objectives are. It is the sum of both its stated aims, policies and practice, and what it actually does and achieves. It may or may not reflect what it would like to be.

Institutional identity

This is the image the institution would like to have and to present to its various internal and external audiences. It will be the creative product of a planning process and designed to support and facilitate the achievement of the organization's goals.

Visual identity

This is one part of an institution's identity, and refers to those elements that are visual: written communications, publicity, whether as literature or in audio-visual form, the appearance of people within the organization, and the institution's plant – its buildings, vehicles and signs. A common feature of visual identity may well be the use of a device representing the school, such as a crest or logo. In addition, a common tool is the use of a particular typeface or font in which to write the institution's name, and such a device is known as a logotype.

Olins (1989) expresses the idea of an organization's identity well:

> In order to be effective every organisation needs a clear sense of purpose that people within it understand. They also need a strong sense of belonging. Purpose and belonging are the two facets of identity. Every organisation is unique, and the identity must spring from the organisation's own roots, its personality, its strengths and its weaknesses. . . . The identity of the [organisation] must be so clear that it becomes the yardstick against which its products, behaviour and actions are measured. This means that the identity cannot simply be a slogan, a collection of phrases; it must be visible, tangible and all-embracing.
>
> (Olins 1989:7)

It is clear that Olins regards institutional identity as being the focus of a process of internal motivation for the organization, and that the external image and identity arise naturally from this. Substantial expenditure on a new logo is wasted money if the logo does not reflect an institutional personality that either does not exist or cannot be achieved. Indeed, one of the first purposes of an institutional identity programme may well be the conversion of staff to understand its message and advantages, and this reflects the almost classic view of Peters and Waterman: 'Excellent organisations create environments in which people can blossom, develop self-esteem and be excited participants in the organisation and society as a whole' (Peters and Waterman 1982:4).

It is possible to identify four aspects of a school's activity in which institutional identity is reflected.

1   The educational service provided. This relates to all aspects of the work of the school or college. It includes the design and delivery of the curriculum, and the administrative, support and managerial processes in the school.

2   The nature of the school environment. This relates to the physical environment of the school and includes the working environment of pupils or students, the work environment of all staff, the recreational and leisure environment for all who work there, and the public areas where external visitors may be met. Issues such as carpeting, decorative order, the presence of regularly changed display material and the use of plants and lighting are all important in portraying the image. Clear, consistent and attractive signing systems are also an important feature.

3   The provision of information. This relates to all aspects of communication and includes everyday communications as reflected in letterheads, compliment slips, memos and forms, and the regular publications, including the prospectus, and staff, student and parent handbooks. Beyond this it extends to advertising materials and the livery of school vehicles. Important is the recognition that both the medium and the message are ingredients of information flow. An excellent institution will fail to communicate its virtues without careful consideration of its methods. Equally, a slick presentational style will not, in the long run, prevent the fundamental deficiencies of a school or college from becoming apparent.

4   Behaviour and relationships. This relates to the way in which the people within the organization behave towards each other, towards the institution and towards those from outside the school or college. Every communication by every member of staff at every level, and by every pupil or student, is part of the institution's external relations programme whether they are aware of it or not.

NAMES AND LOGOS

A central element of most institutional identity programmes is the major visual representation it uses: its name and its logo or crest.

Both convey a substantial amount of information about a school or college. The use of a crest as opposed to a logo suggests a link with a long and distinguished history, as does the application of a Latin or Greek motto. It implies quality based on experience and standing, with a respect for traditional values. Alternatively, the adoption of a modern logo suggests a focus on the modern world, an institution of the 1990s. It is enlightening to consider a range of logos and symbols to try to gain some insight into the purpose of the symbolization (Figure 12.1).

The same applies to names. Names are part of an institution's personality, and imply particular values and associations. It is difficult to accept the axiom that 'a rose by any other name would smell as sweet' when it comes to school names. Governors in many schools will have discussed the virtues of a name change with the intention of altering an undesirable image.

THE PURPOSE OF AN INSTITUTIONAL IDENTITY PROGRAMME

So why bother with developing an institutional identity programme (IIP)? What benefits will it bring to a school or college that will offset the inevitable costs that will be incurred in its creation? The IIP will bring one set of advantages in itself, while the visual identity programme (VIP), which will be part of the IIP, will confer its own range of benefits.

Perhaps the major advantage of the IIP comes from the process of development in itself. As institutional identity stems from the nature and aims of the organization, it requires a fundamental analysis of what those aims are. The existence of a primary aim or mission statement for a school is to be found on the first page of most prospectuses. Of key importance, however, is how that aim is conveyed through the actions, attitudes, policies, management processes and communications of the school. The second virtue of an IIP is that it requires an institution to focus on how it operates in every dimension. Every process in the school has an outcome with an image dimension to it and every one of these processes needs to be examined to identify what its image facet is, what image it portrays and whether this reinforces or contradicts the aims of the institution.

A third advantage lies in the necessity of examining how the institution is perceived by its external audiences. Identifying the

HARRIS   CITY   TECHNOLOGY   COLLEGE
Maberley Road, London SE19 2JH
Tel: 081-771 2261 Fax: 081-771 7531

THE CROSSLEY HEATH SCHOOL

CHOSEN HILL SCHOOL
Brookfield Road, Churchdown, Gloucester. GL3 2PL
Telephone (0452) 713488 FAX 0452 714976

Headteacher: A. Winwood, B.A., M.Ed.

TAUNTON
SCHOOL

Figure 12.1 Some examples of institutional identity as expressed through crests and logos

perceptions of these groups is a major task of research, but can be clearly enlightening, and it is here that the match or mismatch between the desired image and the reality emerges.

A fourth advantage of an IIP relates to its potential unifying effect. It would be naïve to believe that all members of an organization will agree with its stated aims or the management processes it operates, but staff generally value the sense of belonging that comes from being part of an institution with clear aims and a clear identity.

The usual outcome of an IIP has two facets: a staff development programme and a visual identity programme (VIP). The former is intended to precipitate the benefits outlined in earlier paragraphs. It is worth considering here the benefits of a VIP.

1   Projects coherence and identity. This is the prime purpose of the VIP, in that it conveys through visual communications the idea of the prime aim of the institution and its character, purpose and *modus operandi*. It suggests an institution where management is strong and efficient, and where personnel in the school are working towards common goals.

2   Presents confidence and style. This suggests that the organization is confident in both the value of its aims and its ability to achieve them.

3   Helps the school become better known. The constant association of an eye-catching visual image with the institution is bound to make it more easily recognized and better known in the community.

4   Provides promotional benefits. This may be perceived as the primary aim of a VIP, in that it draws in more applicants for student/pupil places or staff appointments, or that it attracts practical and financial support from outside organizations. This may come from the image itself, or through the view that a school that cares about its image is essentially a client-centred institution.

5   Saves time and effort in the long term. Developing a VIP is time-consuming in the short term, but particularly in large schools and colleges the possession of standard means of presenting ideas and information to outside organizations can save time and money.

Moving towards the development of an IIP may, of course, not be a smooth process. The cost implications may be substantial in the early stages if the use of external advisors and a professional designer is to be considered. In addition, the time commitment in undertaking client research, briefing designers, evaluating proposals and initiating new systems may be substantial. The costs of introducing the new programme may also be significant – for example, the production of new signage, new notepaper and new furnishings for a reception area. Staff development may also raise challenges of time and money. Clearly, cost economies may be made by internal servicing of some of these processes, but the long-term costs of choosing an in-house design must always be considered. Against this, however, needs to be set the benefit of extra income that may be derived from having such a programme. Income from additional pupils or students is large enough to mean that high outgoings may soon be recouped.

A second issue relates to managing the process of change that such a programme brings. No IIP has ever been introduced without generating friction in the system. Most individuals and organizations are 'dynamically conservative', in that they 'fight like mad to remain the same' (Day 1986). In addition, individuals may deploy a wide range of tactics to resist the change that an IIP pushes them towards. An IIP may challenge the identity that individuals attach to the institution and their own role within it. Clearly, this means that an essential part of the IIP is to carry the staff into and through the change that it requires, by a process of positive encouragement and a demonstration of the short-term and long-term benefits.

A third problem may be the failure to recognize that image and personality in institutions are dynamic. An appropriate image for the 1980s may not be an appropriate image for the 1990s. Fashion in visual identity will also change. Perhaps it is reasonable to think of institutional identity as having a life cycle in the same way that commercial organizations identify product life cycles. What this means for schools and colleges is that there is a need for constant evaluation of institutional identity, and for an individual or group to monitor the IIP and make recommendations for modification, fundamental change or complete replacement as appropriate.

CREATING AN INSTITUTIONAL IDENTITY PROGRAMME

The process of creating an institutional identity has tended to be somewhat idiosyncratic in the past. It may well have been the product of the ideas of the first headteacher in the school, and will reflect that individual rather than a clear plan of image creation and management. If the image is to be effective, it must be the outcome of a structured plan and process, which in turn are part of the whole external relations planning programme of the school (see Chapter 1). It is possible to identify a number of clear stages in the process. These reflect the views of Keen and Greenall (1987), and Keen and Warner (1989), but have been modified here to make them reflect the needs of schools.

Stage 1: The identity audit

This audit may be the responsibility of a single member of the institution's own staff, or a small working group. Alternatively, it may be appropriate to engage an external consultant. This latter course has the advantage of providing objectivity to the process by introducing an individual with a wide understanding of the issues. In addition, as the process involves gaining insights and perceptions from current staff and students or pupils it removes any sense of threat they may feel. The identity audit itself revolves around a series of key questions.

1 Who or what are the internal and external audiences that are likely to have an image of the institution?
2 What are the main characteristics of the image the institution conveys to each of its audiences?
3 What are the consequences for the institution of the image portrayed?
4 What are the short-term and long-term aims and priorities of the institution?
5 What is the current nature of the institution's visual identity? What logo, symbol, crest and colours are used, and how are they used? Do they match the aims of the institution? What is the appearance of the buildings and plant like, and what image does it convey?

Stage 2: Comparison

This involves examining the image of other schools and colleges. The aim is to identify their strengths and weaknesses, opportunities and threats, but it also enables the identification of good practice, and the recognition of an 'image niche' that may be unexploited as yet.

Stage 3: Consultation

This involves discussion with all internal audiences to glean ideas about what the visual identity might be and the practical issues involved. Those responsible for any facet of external communication will have clear views on the practical aspects of a VIP, and may well have ideas on form and style.

Stage 4: Design

The design process may be undertaken either 'in-house' or by external designers. The results of Stages 1–3 should provide the basis of a design brief, from which a number of proposals might be generated. The starting point for the designers may be the generation of an institutional logo, which in turn may drive other aspects of the IIP. An effective institutional logo will have a number of characteristics: distinctiveness; ready association with the institution; compatibility with the institution's external relations strategy; simplicity; adaptability, that is, the capacity to be used in a number of controlled ways; attractiveness; and durability, in that for economic reasons it needs to have as long a potential life cycle as possible.

Stage 5: The proposal

The finalized ideas need to be considered by senior management and the governing body, along with a costed implementation plan.

Stage 6: Implementation

Practical implementation requires a time-linked sequence of activities that will enable the new identity to be installed. Some changes may be achievable in the very short-term, for example, the printing of new headed notepaper when stocks run out, but others will need a longer lead time. Changes to school uniform, for example, can only be introduced over a period of time. The staff development programme may have a higher priority within the implementation, for it is only with the involvement and commitment of the staff that the programme can get off the ground. Initial presentation of the programme and its *raison d'être* will certainly be necessary. 'Front-of-house' training for all those involved in direct communication with external audiences may also be an early requirement.

Stage 7: Monitoring and evaluation

As with all aspects of development in school, a key element is evaluating the progress of the project and the impact of its introduction. This may be seen at two levels. First, it is essential to check that the IIP is implemented in the correct way and in a way that is as efficient as possible. Second, the evaluation requires a systematic review of the changes that the programme brings about and their value to the school. Changes in attitudes and perceptions by internal and external audiences will also give clear feedback on the programme, and will serve to give direction to the manipulation and modification of the IIP.

CASE STUDIES

To examine the purpose and management of IIPs it is instructive to examine two case studies of change in relation to institutional identity.

Crestwood Community School

Crestwood Community School is a mixed 11–16 school in Eastleigh, Hampshire, with a roll of about 600 pupils. Its catchment area is fairly mixed in socio-economic terms. In January 1989 a new headteacher, Mrs V. Morley, was appointed, and one of the aspects of the school that she believed needed consideration was its image. No formal process of institutional identity planning or evaluation has been undertaken, but a steady review of image has resulted in a number of clear changes.

Crestwood _{SCHOOL}

CRESTWOOD COMMUNITY SCHOOL

SHAKESPEARE ROAD · EASTLEIGH · HANTS · SO5 4FZ · 0703 · 641232

Figure 12.2 Crestwood School – institutional identity

1 A review of the school's corporate image was undertaken by a working party of staff volunteers. A variety of name ideas and logos was considered before the focus on the name Crestwood was chosen (Figure 12.2). This process included buying in the services of design and identity consultants on a very small budget for half a day's work, but the final ideas were generated internally within the school. The new identity has been incorporated extensively into the literature of the school.

2 The second focus of interest related to school uniform. Prior to 1989, the school had a limited dress code for pupils, and the new headteacher sought to develop a flexible but much more structured uniform. This was partly to project the school's image in the local community and also because of a belief that 'looking smart encourages acting smart'. Parents were asked for comments after the idea had been raised, and there was only limited resistance. The scheme was phased in over two years to avoid a major expenditure impact on parents.

3 The design of the building for both school and community use made access for visitors fairly difficult, so the next stage was to enhance signage and the reception area. With only limited expenditure a quiet and warm waiting room was created to replace the previous system of visitors waiting in the corridor.

4 The importance of parents as partners in the school was recognized through two specific projects. First, homework diaries were replaced by personal record books, which were much wider in scope and enabled a continuing dialogue between parents, pupils and teachers to take place. Second, a newsletter was introduced,

which ensured that parents were kept abreast of current developments and activities in the school.

5 A final area of activity related to tackling the litter problem.
Tutor groups are assigned to duty weeks to keep the inside and
outside of the buildings litter-free, and the school's concern for
this area of identity is reflected in its designation of the care-
takers as 'building superintendents', with a responsibility for
concern for the physical environment written into their job
description.

The process of development of the institutional image and identity
has clearly been well received by staff and parents, and is seen as
only the initial stage in a longer programme. The headteacher
would like to move towards the designation of a member of staff
with particular design interests to take a central co-ordinating role
in all visual identity issues. In addition, she would like to raise
the standard of classroom visual appearance to reflect a more
corporate style and a greater concern for the visual environment.
The headteacher sees the creation of staff support as both a managerial challenge and one of her major roles in the process. By
encouraging ownership of ideas, change is portrayed as growth,
but this can only happen where the overall management style is
open and consultative. Furthermore, she believes strongly that
identity and image have to be generated from within, for 'if they
are peripheral or imposed they will whither away'.

Chandlers Ford Junior School

Chandlers Ford Junior School is situated close to the centre of
Chandlers Ford, a commuter town for the Southampton conur-
bation. The school, built in the 1950s, has a roll of 360–90. Its
catchment is mostly from professional families, providing what
the headteacher, Mr D. A. Sergeant, describes as 'well-motivated
children, and an active, supportive parents' association'. The
school's interest in developing its image and identity arose during
1990–1 in response to two stimuli: the arrival of Mr Sergeant as
a new headteacher in September 1990, and the construction of a
new junior school to open in September 1991 on the edge of the
school's catchment area, which provides direct competition for
recruitment of pupils.

The image programme has developed on an *ad hoc* basis in

response to opportunity and perceived priorities. This is the result of an absence of resources, particularly time, for sophisticated institutional planning and the need to progress at a pace the school, the pupils and the parents can respond to. The programme has seen a number of developments.

1 On joining the staff, the headteacher perceived the extensive and varied grounds as being 'sterile and under-used'. With the support of the parents' association and the Learning through Landscapes Trust, and the free help of a college student who undertook the design work as part of a project, the school has created a pond, developed an area of coppiced woodland as a nature reserve and undertaken an extensive programme of planting.

2 The lack of appropriate signage and a welcoming appearance for visitors had been a perceived problem in September 1990. With the help of a grant from the LEA to upgrade office equipment, and the provision of self-help building by parents and staff, the whole reception area was upgraded substantially.

3 Wider improvements to the school buildings were made possible by providing money from the school's own budget to pay for the caretaker, re-designated the site officer, to spend six hours each week doing odd jobs. In addition, the school is raising money through the virement of £20,000 from the 1990–91 budget to the 1991–92 budget and through the contribution of about £10,000 from the LEA minor works budget to pay for the building of a new resources centre and library. This improved facility will release two classrooms previously used for the purpose and allow two temporary classrooms to be removed from the site.

4 In support of the creation of the new image from these developments, the headteacher felt strongly that a name change for the school was also appropriate, along with the design of a logo. Despite its formal name the school is known locally as Merdon School or Merdon Avenue School because of its location in Merdon Avenue. Local research revealed that the coppiced woodland was one of the last vestiges of the ancient Merdon woodland owned by Merdon Castle some 5 miles distant, and that the school stands on the site of an old clay pit which provided the bricks for Merdon Castle. In response to these historical links and ideas the headteacher made a proposal to the governors that the name should be formally changed to

Figure 12.3 Merdon Junior School – institutional identity

Merdon Junior School from September 1991. To support the name change the headteacher sought to introduce a crest or logo. Using a symbol found in the ancient Merdon Castle accounts, one of the parents who was a graphic design artist produced a new logo (Figure 12.3), which was approved by a governors' sub-committee.

The headteacher indicates that the response from within the school has been very positive to all the changes, and that the parents' association is 'thrilled'. The changes have been achieved within tight budgetary constraints, but substantial progress has been made in the space of one year. Although no formal monitoring of the change in image and perception is planned, the headteacher believes that the school community now has a sense of ownership of the school, and a real sense of local history. In particular, though, the major pay-off has been the enhancement of the already good links with parents.

CONCLUSION

Institutional identity is a growing concern among governors and headteachers. Despite the link in the minds of many in education between image and hype or intentional, manipulative deceit, the value of an effective institutional identity programme is increasingly being recognized. Pay-offs are to be found in both enhanced recruitment of staff and students or pupils, and also in the facilitation of the institution's external relations. Perhaps of more immediate and impressive value is the enhancement of internal relationships and the potential of this for distilling a more unified sense of purpose. As a final word, however, it is worth noting the three key principles that Keen and Greenall (1987) suggest must underlie all planning of external relations, and which apply particularly to considerations of institutional identity.

1 Worcester's Law: familiarity breeds favourability, rather than contempt, and hence an image that is well projected and reaches the external audiences frequently and effectively will enhance the institution's reputation.
2 No institution can, in the long run, obtain a good reputation unless it deserves to have one. The projection of an image that does not reflect reality will eventually undermine the institution's credibility.
3 Quality does not necessarily speak for itself. Institutions need to ensure that the personality and image of the school or college are carefully managed and communicated to external audiences.

Chapter 13

Marketing the school as an educational institution

Lynton Gray

Marketing is a central management task in any organization. Every school benefits from the careful examination of the needs of its clients and customers, and from the resulting efforts to meet those needs more precisely. Services such as the education service are particularly vulnerable when they fail to listen to their customers, and schools need to reflect upon their relationships with both their customers and those who sponsor them, starting from the recognition that those who use their services are customers with needs, rights and expectations.

Marketing is not an alien concept, dredged from the more unsavoury corners of the business world and imposed upon unwilling schools. Instead, it is a set of ideas and activities that help schools to improve educational provision and practice. Where marketing becomes integrated as a central aspect of school management, the other elements of management are improved. This chapter emphasizes that careful planning is the essence of effective marketing and suggests some ways in which schools might look at their existing marketing and public relations practices in order to make them even more effective.

Until recently, many thought that marketing had no place in schools; but not so long ago they also thought that there was no place for management either. Schools have always marketed themselves, although those which led this aspect of the school's work have done so instinctively, with little or no formal organization, minimal expenditure and no knowledge of or reference to those principles of marketing that shape the marketing operations of industrial and commercial organizations. This is now changing rapidly. Schools now look to marketing in order to increase their resources, or at least to compensate for resource reductions. A marketing perspective also helps schools recognize that, unless questions of quality of service are addressed, those extra resources are unlikely to be forthcoming.

Interest in the marketing of schools and their educational services has been stimulated by central government activities over the past decade. A basic government objective has been to improve the efficiency of the public sector by increasing competition. This was one purpose of the Education Reform Act 1988, which sought to provide greater choice for parents by driving schools into more competitive stances and by removing those local authority policies that sought to achieve 'value for money' by the alternative route of planned provision. The consequence of these policies has been to inject a number of features of a market economy into public sector education. Two new categories of schools have been established to compete with local authority-provided schools: city technology colleges and grant-maintained schools, both funded directly from the DES/DFE.

Underlying and intensifying all this government-promoted competition has been the impact of major demographic change. The total population of young people in Britain has declined by up to one-third since the 1970s. Schools either had to compete for a reduced number of potential customers or face contraction or even closure. By and large, schools have generally managed to avoid closure, with the result that institutions are now generally smaller and more competitive than they were a decade ago. The 1988 legislation has made it even easier to resist planned closure, by offering schools the opportunity to opt out of local authority control. Market forces have, in consequence, replaced local government planning as the prime means by which educational provision might be geared to the needs and numbers of education's customers.

A fundamental belief that the school is there to provide a service, and to respond to the needs of its pupils and their parents and employers, lies at the heart of effective marketing. The myth that the professionals within the education service were uniquely qualified to identify and express those needs has been exploded, not only by the Education Reform Act 1988 and its Scottish and Northern Irish equivalents, but by more deep-seated changes in the relationships between the teachers, school support staff and their customers. A more systematic approach to the marketing of educational provision is an inevitable response to demographic change and to social shifts in which the consumers of both public and private services recognize their rights and are more ready to insist that their expectations are met. Increased competition and customer care in the public sector are not just short-term responses to government policies.

It is important to emphasize from the outset that marketing is a great deal more than the advertising and other selling activities that many people associate with it. A marketing perspective is, therefore, a lot more than the encouragement of unbridled competition, using unsavoury sales techniques. Indeed, collaboration is also an important aspect of marketing the school. In some areas schools have banded together in order to promote their service collectively: for example, Avon's secondary schools have hired a public relations agency to help them promote their strengths, including the ways in which schools co-operate to improve their service through consortia.

The National Association of Head Teachers has published a code of conduct for all its members, to encourage such collaboration (NAHT 1990). This defines and seeks to proscribe 'unprofessional activities', including the offer of inducements such as gifts and commercial incentives to prospective pupils, the reporting of examination results in ways that undermine rival schools and the use of money from teaching funds on marketing activities. The code states that its members should take account of the effects of their marketing activities on neighbouring schools.

Local authorities have shown similar concerns that marketing does not degenerate into destructive competition. Warwickshire has published a voluntary code of conduct for its schools, which proposes constraints upon the distribution of publicity materials and strongly discourages any comparisons between schools, whether in publicity materials and advertising or in public meetings.

THE MARKETING PERSPECTIVE

In successful service organizations, a distinctive marketing orientation is readily identifiable. It is based upon attitudes, backed by activities, which give pre-eminence to the organization's customers. These attitudes are reflected in the way in which the enterprise is organized and managed. A marketing orientation in schools is, therefore, one in which the interests and needs of the pupil as customer are central. Other clients – notably employers and parents – are also recognized, and due attention is given to their concerns and needs. These needs are regarded as the central reason for the school's existence, and are recognized as even more important than the needs of its staff or governors.

Central to the marketing of any educational service must be a concern for the nature and the quality of the curriculum. A school marketing strategy must, therefore, both take account of the curriculum and attempt to influence it. Schools could well benefit from a closer examination from a marketing perspective of the curriculum choices available to their students, including the teaching and learning processes they are expected to undertake. The standardization imposed by a National Curriculum might be countered by a stronger emphasis upon the quality of learning opportunities and the individualization of learning. In an increasingly competitive environment, schools will need to identify responses attractive to potential clients, which emphasize the quality of curriculum provision rather than any distinctive content. They then need to develop strategies for drawing customers' attention to this.

A marketing perspective must contain centrally within it the clear recognition that the public service should be available to satisfy the needs of all its publics. This includes those groups traditionally disadvantaged in their access to high-quality education. Marketing is a vital means by which such groups are first made aware of the opportunities available to them and then helped to make full use of the services thus provided. Any equal opportunities policy must have a marketing dimension – and vice versa.

This perspective focuses upon customers and services and is largely but not only, concerned with customer satisfaction. A school marketing perspective is also concerned with ways in which existing services meet national, local and community expectations and needs, and, in particular, the needs of groups which have traditionally underachieved at school. The concern with customer satisfaction includes the encouragement and promotion of the view that educational provision is a matter not just of current consumption – a major component of user satisfaction – but is also an investment in the future.

This is delivered through appropriate organization and management. The organizational structures are designed around customers and their needs, rather than on sub-divisions representing factional interests and staff wishes. The management processes focus on the delivery of quality services, and emphasize the provision of those rewards and controls that ensure that attention is concentrated on service delivery as efficiently and effectively as possible. In order to do this – usually with limited resources – these management processes need to integrate resources, staff capabilities and customer needs in ways that use minimal resources for maximum effect. This is not going to happen just because of the charisma or intuition of the managers, or the good intentions of the staff. Careful planning is needed to ensure that the organization's marketing, resource and curriculum objectives are achieved. Management needs to operate in the context of a carefully worked through marketing plan.

In order to achieve planned outcomes a number of specific techniques and tactics are needed. One element of the marketing plan should be the careful improvement of the organization's capacity to operate these techniques and undertake these tactics skilfully to the benefit of the customer.

UNDERSTANDING THE MARKET

Before any marketing strategy or plan can be determined, knowledge of the market to be served is essential. Any market comprises a range of products or services and groups of customers, actual and potential. Public sector schools are not free to offer services of their choice to customers of their choice: indeed, the introduction of a National Curriculum has reduced this freedom. Schools were set up and funded for specific purposes involving pupils (customers) specified by age group, and often by ability and geographical location. It is necessary for schools to examine the market in which they operate, however imperfectly that market functions. This, in turn, requires information, which comes into two broad categories: the need to analyse information already available, whether within or outside the school; and information not as yet collected.

In the first case, some ordering and analysis of existing information are required, involving a *marketing audit* (Gray 1991). Schools are awash with information, collected for purposes other than marketing and organized in ways that make it difficult to provide information for marketing activities. It is possible, however, to re-order and analyse this data to make it more useful. The quest for information not currently available requires the rather different approach of *marketing research* (see Davies and Scribbins 1985). This involves the collection, analysis and interpretation of information specifically collected for marketing purposes. It needs to be well planned and organized, but need not be an expensive activity: indeed, it can form part of the curriculum activities within the school.

PLANNING FOR MARKETING

Information from the marketing audit and marketing research needs to be assembled and analysed so as to provide a basis for planning. It needs to be considered alongside the mission, goals and agreed objectives already established for the organization. Schools, like other public sector organizations, must include here those objectives set by central government nationally and by the local authority or other 'owners' (the governing body) locally.

One simple framework for the assembly and analysis of market information is the well-tried SWOT analysis. Its title is taken from the capital letters of the four cells shown in Figure 13.1. Analysis of the upper two cells is based upon the careful examination of the strengths and weaknesses of the institution. The lower two cells use evidence from the external environment in order to consider the opportunities and threats facing the school. Evidence for the SWOT analysis can be found in files and records, and through the experience and knowledge of staff and pupils.

The assembly and analysis of information are a central and essential basis for the planning process. The outcome should be a *marketing plan*. This lies at the heart of the effective organization of educational marketing. This is not a separate planning activity, but forms part of the broader school development plan. The plan needs to take available information, ideas and policies and turn them into proposals for action. The classic structure for organizing such action in marketing is referred to as the '*marketing mix*'. This has five components when applied to service industries like education, known as the *five Ps*: product, place, price, promotion and people (Figure 13.2). These are the variables that can be controlled and adjusted by organizations in order to produce a blend that represents their preferred marketing stance. This simple and powerful notion is central to most marketing textbooks, including those focusing upon educational marketing (Gray 1991), and training programmes.

STRENGTHS	WEAKNESSES
OPPORTUNITIES	THREATS

Figure 13.1 Framework for a SWOT analysis

PRODUCT	The goods or services being offered to the market
PLACE	The location and accessibility of the goods/services
PRICE	The resources needed by customers to obtain the goods/services
PROMOTION	The activities communicating the benefits of the goods/services to potential customers
PEOPLE	Those involved in selling and performing the service, and the instruction of customers receiving the service

Figure 13.2 The marketing mix

The notion of a mission statement is central to the planning process and is reflected in the positive image of the school promoted through its marketing. Marketing devices such as the use of a logo, school uniform or high standards of out-of-school behaviour all play their part in this. Careful public relations, including a well-thought-out media relations strategy, also contribute.

Basic marketing principles are important here: clearly identifying the market segments and their needs, and deciding which of those needs can be met; preparing marketing strategies that integrate all elements of the marketing mix and project the messages to customers about the services available from and through the school; and ensuring that the messages going out from existing staff and students are positive. Of course, these messages must be backed by action in the institution to ensure that public relations promises are borne out by the realities of the customers' educational experiences.

If marketing is to be effective it must be closely integrated with the other elements of school management: staff or personnel management; curriculum management; and resource management. Marketing requires resources, but is also an essential means of acquiring resources. The marketing mix approach assists with the examination of the deployment and redeployment of resources. It requires consideration of the relative investment in:

1 promotional techniques, including publicity materials, media relations and advertising;
2 the curriculum and teaching/learning strategies, and, most importantly, the benefits thus accrued – the product or service;
3 the environment in which the service is delivered – the place;
4 the price asked of participants taking up these educational services, including, for students outside public-sector schools, the fees and other expenses, as well as the opportunity costs to students choosing to buy education rather than spend their time and money elsewhere; and
5 people costs, including staff development, training, organization and motivation.

An educational marketing strategy should, therefore, carry a price tag. A marketing audit should identify current resource deployment and research findings may well suggest ways in which the same resources might be deployed more effectively. Torrington and Weightman (1989) have drawn attention to the considerable resource management skills of so many education managers. The marketing plan can then indicate ways in which resources might be both allocated and mobilized in order to achieve the institution's objectives.

Marketing strategies need to be directed internally as much as externally: persuading one's own colleagues of the school's virtues can be far harder than persuading customers. From a marketing perspective, all staff should be encouraged to recognize that they, individually, have marketing responsibilities. These include promoting the school's image and monitoring customer satisfaction, as well as carrying out their central tasks in response to and designed around customer needs. Part of these responsibilities should include shaping customer perceptions so that they recognize and respond not only to the quality of the teaching, but also to the likely benefits arising from learning experiences. These benefits are both the immediate satisfactions of the teaching and learning being undertaken and the longer-term satisfactions achieved only when the benefits of an investment in education are reaped. This should be a life-long process.

An effective marketing strategy should seek to influence the social as well as the educational encounters at school. The activities of non-teaching staff can be as significant as those of the teachers, and the overall ambience of the institution is also important. A marketing perspective should heighten teaching and non-teaching staff awareness of their roles in marketing the school services from the office, reception desk, telephone switchboard and the caretaker's office, as well as from the classroom. This requires investment in staff development and training. Despite the impact of falling rolls throughout the education service, and the consequent threats to job security, teachers and non-teaching staff all too often do not perceive pupils as customers, whose patronage is needed if they are to hold on to their jobs.

PUBLICIZING THE SCHOOL

The preparation of publicity materials by schools and colleges is now well established as a cyclical activity. All schools are required to produce annual brochures and handbooks, and many have become expert at achieving high quality at low cost. The legal and organizational aspects of such publications are considered in detail in Chapter 8.

The preparation of effective educational publicity materials requires, most importantly, honesty. West Sussex trading standards officers once reported that eight private schools had made a total of fifteen bogus claims about their academic achievements and sports facilities. Even if dishonest claims are not picked up by independent watchdogs, they will certainly lead to dissatisfied customers and a damaged reputation. Effective publicity materials spell out the educational vision and mission of the school, with the further benefit that existing staff and students can be helped to recognize that vision more clearly and then promote it.

In designing effective materials, it is necessary to identify precisely the services being promoted, the target audiences, the images to be projected and the reasons why, and the vehicles by which materials will be distributed. In selecting the messages to be projected, care should be taken to ensure that:

1 text is used sparingly, is written clearly and is jargon-free;
2 the use of space and headings is planned carefully, with expert graphic design help – the costs are slight in relation to the impact gained from good presentation;
3 graphics are used selectively;
4 sketches and photographs are prepared with care, by creative talents;
5 the unique selling proposition is clearly spelled out; and
6 the institution's identity is emphasized with the use of a distinctive logo or other repeated device for underlining its distinctiveness.

Some schools recognize the impact that video images have on their prospective customers and, despite the expense, commission the preparation of promotional videos. The advent of the Camcorder makes it possible for schools to prepare these themselves. Other schools put together, at lower cost, audio-visual presentations for use at promotional events and on visits to feeder schools. Schools are usually rich in many of the talents needed here: the clear diction and presentation skills of many teachers can combine with the design and artwork skills of art departments, and the photographic talents often found in the staffroom, to produce attractive and high-quality promotional materials in-house. The acquisition of desktop publishing facilities provides further opportunities for developing, at relatively low-cost, high-quality publicity materials, as long as it is recognized that technology is not a substitute for creative talent.

Direct mail is a useful way of reaching carefully targeted market segments. Traditionally, schools have used their own pupils as unpaid postal workers, delivering dispatches to their own homes and, on occasions, to neighbours. Publicity materials can be distributed in this way to prospective customers with the co-operation of feeder schools. It is usually cost-effective for schools to establish and maintain computerized mailing lists, now that most have computers to manage their delegated finances.

Another useful strategy for drawing the attention of large numbers of people to an educational service is to obtain the agreement of local supermarkets, banks and libraries to display leaflets and other publicity materials – often along with an attractive presentation of artwork by the institution's students. This brightens up the environment and draws attention to the providing school or college.

CONCLUSIONS: ORGANIZING FOR MARKETING

A marketing perspective needs to infuse all corners of the school and involve all staff. The marketing function is a necessary element of the management of educational institutions. In keeping with the growing formalization of school development planning, the organization of educational marketing should include the following:

1 the establishment of marketing objectives and an organizational framework for marketing;
2 the systematic collection of marketing information through marketing audit and research;
3 the development of a costed marketing plan that forms part of the school's corporate plan; and
4 the implementation and evaluation of the strategies and tactics agreed in the plan.

This does no more than redirect a well-tried and long-established approach to the management of education. Underlying it is the fundamental belief that the school is there to provide a service, and to respond to the needs of its pupils and their parents and employers. Sound educational practice has long emphasized collegial responsiveness to student needs. A marketing perspective presents opportunities to listen all the more carefully to the views of students and to those who speak and act on their behalf, to respond effectively to criticisms and to emphasize student choice in the face of the constraints imposed, for example, by the National Curriculum. Marketing emphasizes the need for sound organization and for collegial approaches by teaching and non-teaching staff. Their involvement in and commitment to educational marketing will determine whether or not an educational institution succeeds – or even survives.

Finally, the required marketing skills include the redirection of some basic teaching skills, involving effective communication through a variety of media, tailored to customers whose needs have been carefully and skilfully analysed. Good marketing practice amounts to sound educational practice spiced by the adaptation of approaches effective in the marketing of other services. Schools now need to integrate these practices as central features of institutional management.

Chapter 14

Marketing the school's facilities

Michael Ives

An industrialist would not be impressed with the use most schools make of their plant, buildings and grounds. Normal school use of such assets – five days a week, seven hours a day and thirty-nine weeks in a full year – would spell financial disaster for most commercial undertakings. With the advent of LMS, maintained schools have joined the independent sector in controlling their own budgets. Budgets not only apportion expenditure but also project future income. Income to schools depends on pupil population and any other income that can be generated to maximize revenue. There is considerable scope for making full commercial use of school facilities to generate additional revenue, but when considering the attraction of such projects it should always be remembered that a school's primary and overriding duty is the education of its own pupils.

Many schools will already have established links with groups paying for the use of grounds or classrooms. They may already have enterprise projects with farms or greenhouses. Yet, if meaningful income is to be derived from the use of school facilities, proper consultation and planning need to be carried out so that the income can be maximized with minimal disruption to the school, its staff and pupils.

ASSESSING THE POTENTIAL

In an initial survey, or audit, a small team needs to evaluate the school's resources for commercial use and profit, with members drawn from the school staff, both teaching and administrative, the governing body and the PTA. The selection of the group members should be based on their knowledge of the school and their ability to demonstrate imaginative thought or entrepreneurial flair. The aim of this group is to make clear proposals for an appropriate strategy. A preliminary paper setting out ideas should be prepared for consultation with staff and, after further refinement, placed before the governing body for its approval. The topics that will need to be examined might include the following areas.

School facilities

A full list of facilities grouped under defined areas of the school campus needs to be compiled (Figure 14.1). A methodical approach will ensure that under-used or under-appreciated facilities belonging to the school are not overlooked. An abandoned pavilion may be of use to a visiting football team or a potting shed to a gardening club!

Possible activities

A list of potential activities should be drawn up and set against the areas of the campus that might be available for commercial use. Imagination should be given free rein as a market can be created from an innovative idea – for example, a Saturday fun morning for children in the sports hall while parents shop can be very popular in a city centre but may not be feasible in a rural area (Figure 14.2).

Potential clients

During the planning and consultation phase, organizations need to be listed under the possible activities. Local knowledge on the part of staff will be useful in compiling a list of potential clients. The library and tourist information centre will have lists of sports clubs and music and drama groups. The local paper will yield advertisements over a period for such activities, which will ultimately provide the market database when active selling of the facilities is undertaken, once the marketing plan has been approved.

BUILDINGS

CLASSROOMS By groups,   DINING HALL/KITCHEN
   number and size

COMMON ROOMS   ASSEMBY HALL

LIBRARY   SPORTS HALL/GYMNASIUM

OUTSIDE AREAS

PLAYING FIELDS   PLAYGROUNDS
   Summer/winter pitches   Access to highway

   Tennis courts

   Specialist facilities   AMENITY GROUND
   such as cricket nets,
   or athletic equipment

                               PAVILIONS AND STORES

Figure 14.1 A simple audit of school facilities

Pricing policy

Most schools in the area will already be making facilities available
to the public for letting purposes. LEAs will have a charging rate
for the use of classrooms or sports facilities. It would seem appropriate that, by agreement between schools, this is used as a base
line for charges. While a price cartel is not to be advocated, a
price war would be highly undesirable.

BUILDINGS

- Drama groups
- Dance schools
- Choirs
- Orchestras
- Education courses
- Recreational courses
- Sports clubs

GROUNDS

- Caravan clubs
- Scout camps, etc
- Car-boot sales
- Car parking
- Overnight parking
- Antique fairs
- Auctions
- Trade and craft fairs

SPORTS FIELDS

- Sports teams
- Archery clubs
- Business hospitality

HOME-GROWN

- Academic courses
- Extra-mural activities
- Sports club

Figure 14.2 Possible activities using school facilities

Administrative and financial arrangements

Full consideration needs to be given to the detailed administration of lettings. The booking would normally be made by a member of the office staff, but oversight by a deputy headteacher or bursar with full knowledge of the school's administration and policy is essential. Liaison may be necessary at this point with members of staff who have an interest in the facility, as any conflict in bookings would be an embarrassment. The school would normally have priority use of its own facilities in term time. A simple system to operate is for all bookings to be displayed on a wall calendar. A separate calendar can be used for each major facility and placed in a convenient public area where staff can consult it before setting a date for their own activities. All bookings should be entered, not only those of outside agencies but also the out-of-hours use by school staff and the PTA.

Some schools have appointed development officers in recent years, whose duties include marketing the school with a view to increasing the market share of pupils, letting the school's facilities and general fund-raising. As a separate appointment this may not be cost-effective initially, but a short-term contract, profit-sharing on a commission only basis or a part-time appointment might be worth investigation. LMS enables schools in the state sector to follow the lead of those in the independent sector in this field.

The raising of invoices can be done by the booking officer or the accounts department. In the initial stages a simple system can be used. When the enterprise develops, further considerations may have to be taken into account. A turnover in excess of £35,000 (1991–2 figures) will necessitate registration with HM Customs and Excise and the charging of VAT. Similarly, if the profits become substantial corporation tax may become payable, at which stage the assistance of professional advisors will be necessary. Accountants may well suggest setting up a limited company that would covenant any profits back to the school, which can reclaim the corporation tax paid if it becomes a registered charity.

Some groups may hire the school facilities on a weekly basis. If the facility is let weekly for at least ten weeks, with agreement to pay for the facility whether used or not, this will constitute a 'licence to occupy' and will, therefore, not be subject to VAT. Figure 14.3 shows an example of a formal licence to occupy.

Letting policy

Guidelines need to be discussed with the governing body as to the propriety of letting premises to particular organizations. Some political activities or religious beliefs may not be deemed commensurate with the aims and objectives of the school. It may be decided, therefore, not to let to any organization with political or religious affiliations or, alternatively, to be circumspect in taking bookings from these organizations and require reference to, for example, the chairperson of governors before granting approval.

There will be occasions when school groups such as the PTA will require the use of facilities. They should book through the usual system, but there should be concessions on charging for the use of the facilities, particularly if the function is a fund-raising activity for the school.

Similarly, charitable organizations may need facilities, but may be reluctant to commit themselves to the full charges in advance in case a loss to the charity is incurred. In this case an informal

LICENCE TO OCCUPY GROUNDS/BUILDINGS
(VAT Notice 701 Exemption Schedule Group 1)

A licence to occupy facilities at .... is granted to

.... Club/Society

for the purpose of ....

in the ....

The period of occupancy will be commencing .... (date)

ending .... (date)* between ....

and .... o'clock on each .... day.
*minimum period three months, excluding school holidays.

The Club/Society shall have exclusive use of the ....

facility for the above period. The charge will be £ .... per ....

The total payment of £ .... due on 19   will be
payable whether the facility is used or not.

The Governors of   shall not be held responsible to the
hirers or their licensees, agents or other persons who at their request
or instigation or who attend functions on the College premises for
any accident happening or any injury suffered or damage or loss of
any chattel or property sustained in any manner whatsoever on any
part of the school premises.

The Governors of   would recommend that the licensees
cover their liabilities to themselves with a suitable insurance policy.

for the Governors of   for

date ....   date ....

Figure 14.3 A specimen licence to occupy school facilities

profit-sharing scheme might be negotiated up to the full charge for the facility, depending upon the takings at the function.

Allocation of profits

There may be resistance to the whole concept of marketing the school's facilities from staff or governors, in which case the profits should be allocated to a specific project that would be unattainable in the normal course of school funding. This should not only secure the backing of the school community, but also give a clear objective to encourage full co-operation from all concerned. The separate accounting procedure will lend itself to monitoring progress towards the attainment of the central objective of the enterprise. At a later stage, when marketing the school's facilities becomes an accepted part of school life, the profits can be taken into the school budget as a reliable profit centre to school income within the general budget forecast.

Licences

The school should already have a theatre licence issued by the local authority. The licence will specify the capacity of the hall, the number of days that it can be used for public entertainment and safety regulations. The Fire Service will inspect the hall to ensure compliance with safety precautions.

Some letting customers may ask to have a bar for the sale of drinks. A policy needs to be formulated to cover this request. While a justice's licence can be obtained, which would licence part of the school for the sale of drink, it may not be considered compatible with the school's ethos. Providing there is no policy objection, the user can be invited to obtain his own occasional licence to operate a bar. This can be done through a local solicitor making an application to the licensing justices. Alternatively, an existing licensee, such as a local landlord, can be invited to operate the bar on a franchise basis. The profit will not be as great, but it avoids either the school or the hirer having to obtain the licence, purchase stock, man the bar and deal with stock control problems.

Insurance

Insurance cover for third party indemnity will be held by every school, whether through the LEA or as a policy taken out by the school itself. Insurers need to be informed that additional activities will take place at the school as a result of a marketing enterprise. There will not normally be an increase in premiums, but insurers must be informed of the intention to widen the use of the school facilities as this will increase the risk that they carry.

ACTIVE MARKETING

Having consulted staff, prepared a policy document and secured the approval of the governing body for setting up a marketing enterprise, further detailed planning for active marketing of the school facilities is required. Many schools have already used their facilities for car-boot sales and sports clubs, but with imagination further enterprises can be devised. Coach and lorry firms have great difficulty in finding overnight parking. City centre schools could use playgrounds at the weekends and during holidays for car parking. Caravan club members often need weekend sites, and a school would be attractive with the use of sports facilities. Corporate entertainment and exhibitions often take place under canvass, and school grounds could provide an attractive location for such events.

Buildings consist of large areas of classrooms. The local college of further education will provide a wide range of courses, but staff members and other instructors from outside the school may have specialized interests that would recruit adult students. They may wish to organize classes in local history, history of art and various handicrafts or skills. The school may hire the room to the instructor rather than become involved in registering students and paying the teacher. Centralized booking and the placement of advertisements could be done on a shared-cost basis. The buildings may lend themselves to drama, dance and music groups, which need space for teaching, rehearsals or productions.

Particular attention needs to be given to planning the best use of a sports hall and any other facilities within a sports complex. There will be sports clubs needing facilities to whom a licence to occupy could be granted. The rentals, based on the LEA rates for such facilities, could be substantial and the administration would not be onerous. However, an alternative method whereby the school operates a sports club may have other advantages, in spite of the higher overheads in the form of employed staff. A well-organized sports club will bring the public and potential pupils into close contact with the school, which would have a positive public relations and marketing impact for future recruitment. The success of the venture depends upon the facilities on offer and the quality of the staff organizing the club.

Those schools that can offer residential accommodation have a distinct advantage in maximizing additional revenue. There are many groups that require holiday-time accommodation coupled with sports or teaching facilities. County orchestras, national youth sports teams, religious groups, language schools and touring sports teams can all be entertained at considerable profit. The Boarding Schools Association publishes a register of schools that offer holiday accommodation, together with charges. Letting during the holidays ensures continuity of employment for catering and cleaning staff. An inclusive charge on a daily basis for accommodation, meals and use of facilities is often made.

CONCLUSION

If marketing the school's facilities is to be a financial success without undue disturbance to the normal school activities, detailed prior planning and the active support of all staff and governors will be essential. Much will depend upon the locality of the school, the entrepreneurial vision of the organizers and the uncomplicated organization of the administration. It is clear that the process will yield a number of benefits to the school that markets its facilities in a successful way. The financial returns may be substantial, but the benefits in terms of other aspects of external relations may be of even greater value. By liaising with many individuals and groups in the community, the school enhances its links with and its perceived value to that community. This, in turn, may well stimulate recruitment of both pupils and staff, and provide opportunities for external links in many curriculum areas.

Chapter 15

Fund-raising from external sources

Gerry Gorman

THE SCALE OF SCHOOL FUND-RAISING

Fund-raising is now an integral part of life for most schools for a variety of reasons, from government cutbacks in educational spending to increased expectations on the part of students, teachers and parents. The introduction of LMS has made school managers more aware of finance, especially because of its uneven effects on different schools. Even those schools that have not suffered disproportionately from the reallocation of resources caused by the advent of LMS are under ever-increasing pressure to obtain those extras that will make the school more attractive to prospective students and their parents.

The combination of these pressures has led many schools to seek funding for items that it was previously regarded as the duty of the LEA to provide:

> At present school funds are being raised for a number of purposes which would in the past have been widely regarded as unacceptable. These include the 'core funding' of teachers' salaries, building repair and maintenance and essential resourcing with books, stationery and teaching equipment. Many parent groups, governing bodies and teachers are still broadly sympathetic to the view that it should not be necessary to raise funds to pay for basic provision. Their dilemma is what to do when faced with evident need for paper, pencils and paint.
>
> (Mountfield 1991:3)

As Mountfield points out, some state schools are beginning to see fund-raising as a means of plugging gaps in government provision. However, given the size of DES/DFE spending on schools relative to the amount that a school can expect to generate, this is likely to be at best a desperate policy.

Estimates of the amounts raised by schools in addition to statutory funding can only be intelligent guesses (Gorman 1988; Mountfield 1991). A reasonable estimate of the non-statutory benefits obtained in cash and donations in kind, including time given by private company staff, would be in the region of £200 million in 1990.

About half this sum would be in cash, suggesting a plausible average non-governmental cash revenue of about £3,000–£4,000 per state school. When this is compared with the typical delegated budget of a quarter of a million pounds for a primary school or a million and a half pounds for a large comprehensive school, it can be seen that even a very successful school is likely to raise only a very small fraction of its income from external sources. In many cases a more thorough marketing effort to attract additional students will be more cost-effective.

OBJECTIONS TO FUND-RAISING

There are many people, both within and outside schools, who have strong and legitimate objections to school fund-raising. These can be divided into two major categories: political or moral objections, and the pressures that fund-raising can place upon pupils, parents and staff.

Many people argue that the state should finance its schools adequately so that they can meet their statutory duties under the various Education Acts. School fund-raising may also reduce the finance available to other charitable causes.

Fund-raising may also put extra pressure on pupils, who already have school work to do and may object to being asked to give up leisure time to raise money. Parents may also grow tired of their children coming home asking for money for one cause or another, and of the major contact with school consisting of what are, effectively, begging letters.

Similarly, teachers are also less likely to be willing unpaid volunteers than they used to be. Understandably, many feel that they are employed primarily to teach, and that other activities such as the administration of the National Curriculum or LMS increasingly crowd out this function.

None of these objections need necessarily deter schools from seeking outside assistance. However, it should always be remembered that pupils, teachers, parents and local people are not a limitless source of time, money and goodwill. Any demands placed upon them should be carefully considered.

MANAGEMENT OF FUND-RAISING

Setting objectives

Fund-raising efforts in schools traditionally have been arranged on an *ad hoc* basis. They are launched, typically, by individual members of staff or departments, with little overall co-ordination or planning. Often this results in failure or causes aggravation to other staff and the local community.

It is vital to set clear objectives for any fund-raising effort. Asking for 'money for the school' is far too vague and unattractive to potential donors. People like to know that their time and money are being used for a specific and worthwhile purpose.

The school should therefore examine the use to which externally raised funds will be put as critically as it considers its income from local or central government. For example, endless hours have been spent by pupils, teachers and parents in raising money for minibuses which have a lower annual mileage than the caretaker's wheelbarrow, or for computers which gather dust between open evenings.

A fund-raising campaign has more chance of success if the organizers can state clearly:

1 what they want to do;
2 by when they are going to do it;
3 if they succeed, what benefits will accrue;
4 what their needs are; and
5 what they have already done towards it.

Ideally, the purpose can be summed up in one or two sentences. If it cannot be expressed concisely it is probably so vague or boring that it does not deserve to succeed.

It is helpful to establish criteria by which the importance and success of a project may be judged. Where possible these should be quantifiable. For example, how many times a week will the minibus leave the school grounds, or how many pupils will have the use of the new science equipment?

Resource implications

Even small fund-raising activities can consume considerable amounts of resources. Some of these, such as materials and renting of halls, will cost money, usually more than expected. Others, such as the time spent by pupils, teachers and parents, are free in the financial sense, but have an opportunity cost in that they take away time that could be used for work or leisure.

Because fund-raising is dependent upon goodwill, schools must be reasonable in their demands upon pupils, staff and parents. Failure to think through this problem will result in people taking on tasks that they cannot achieve. If clear objectives and careful planning are to be implemented, responsibilities must be specified and people's efforts must be recognized, perhaps by extra salary payments.

The standard procedure of forming a committee can be effective if the members are prepared to do more than simply turn up and if the committee has a clear purpose. The most obvious method is to follow the normal administrative procedures of agenda and minutes. Agenda items should be expressed as motions that will lead to action if agreed.

Ultimately, however, responsibility for organization has to rest with a single individual. The traditional approach is to give the job to a deputy headteacher or senior teacher. The main advantage is that this person has high status within the school and with outside bodies, but the disadvantage is that he or she is unlikely to have much time or commitment to any extra responsibility.

There is little point in choosing a co-ordinator without also providing adequate recognition and resources. A small number of schools have appointed a full-time employee specifically to generate funds. This level of funding may be undesirable or impractical, particularly for small schools, but the cost of an incentive allowance and extra non-teaching time should be affordable and recoupable through income generation if the right person is chosen.

CHARITABLE STATUS

If significant amounts of money are to be raised, the school may wish to take advantage of charitable status. Independent and grant-maintained schools are generally registered as charities, but this is not allowed for a state-maintained school.

Although not eligible for charitable status in its own right, a state school can register its fund or PTA for charitable status. Generally, this will be possible if the fund or association provides or helps to provide facilities that are not normally available from the LEA. Details of the conditions and benefits of charitable status can be found in Mountfield (1991), Norton (1988) and Phillips (1988).

LEGAL IMPLICATIONS

Fund-raising activities involve legal and practical problems such as legal responsibilities, handling of money, health and safety, and the arrangement of appropriate insurance. The important principle is: 'if in doubt, consult'. It may be time-consuming and sometimes frustrating trying to get a straight answer from a council official or an insurance company, but no chances should be taken.

Any teacher or other adult who is responsible for supervising children has a duty to take 'reasonable care' of the pupils in their charge. When parents or other adults are to be involved in supervising pupils, they should be accompanied by teachers if possible.

Fund-raising activities often involve people in the use of equipment and materials. Organizers need to consider points such as LEA guidelines, potential hazards, first-aid arrangements, fire regulations and hygiene precautions. Insurance cover must be sufficient to protect organizers against foreseeable problems. The local authority or governing body will have a blanket policy for eventualities such as personal injury and public liability. This is likely to cover governors and employees, but not pupils or other adult helpers. Because of these restrictions, the limitations of insurance policies and the relevant conditions and regulations attached should be checked carefully.

Fund-raising activities often require licences such as those for lotteries and the public performance of music. This requirement is often ignored by schools, which regularly break the law by selling raffle tickets through pupils and playing music at discos.

LARGE-SCALE FUND-RAISING

If the amount needed runs to thousands rather than hundreds of pounds, a more thorough and detailed approach will be needed.

No matter how successful the school disco or sponsored walk may be, for large-scale projects such as hydrotherapy pools or technical workshops help will be needed from large organizations such as charities, businesses or the government. An understanding of how these work and make their decisions can do much to help a school.

There are three main sources of large-scale financial aid: charities and charitable trusts; industry; and government, local and central. As described below, these may have different priorities and require different approaches.

Making contact

Finding potential sources of assistance involves research. Personal contact is important when dealing with external agencies. If assistance is being sought it will help to obtain some idea of the policy of the organization. An informal approach may often save wasted time or increase the chances of a request being granted.

There are several reference books listing possible contacts. These should be available in any good library, and some are cheap and useful enough to make purchase worth while. Before writing, however, it is best to phone and check whether the person named is still in the same job or organization. Asking around may also provide information. Teachers, parents and friends may have personal acquaintances who can provide assistance. A school could also often call upon the services of people such as senior managers of local firms, editors of local papers, councillors and MPs. Publicizing the cause can bring in help from unexpected sources. A special school received several hundred pounds from a karate club whose members had learned of its appeal from a local newspaper. If support can be gained from well-known people it can be used to make an appeal more newsworthy.

If large organizations are approached, or if large sums are involved, the decision-making process may be very slow. Some charities and firms have set times for making such decisions, and may be tied to a particular annual timetable. Some allocate their funds for a year or more at a time. Schools will have to fit in with these policies and plan well in advance.

If help is refused, the particular organization should not be written off altogether. There may be no money available at present, but finance and priorities may change in the future. Unless the organization states that it never supports school activities, it should still be considered for future requests. Sometimes persistence will be rewarded.

Whenever possible, sources of assistance should be acknowledged. This properly recognizes the help that has been given, and also helps to publicize the school's cause.

Writing an application

If the school hopes to gain large-scale assistance, its preparation and approach to potential donors must be professional and commensurate with the amounts requested. Although elaborate documentation may often be inappropriate, any application should contain certain information, such as:

1 basic background information about the school;
2 the amount required and when it is needed;
3 what the money will be spent on;
4 the benefits of the proposed project;
5 the credentials of the school for providing this particular service;
6 why the recipient of the application should support this particular project;
7 other existing or potential donors or supporters; and
8 evidence that the project may have long-term benefits.

Except where more detailed criteria are available, a preliminary request should be kept fairly brief, preferably within two A4 typed pages. Further detailed information can be supplied at a later date if the organization shows an interest in supporting the cause. Applications should also give the impression of being tailored specifically towards the recipient. Although a standard letter may be used, it should be appropriately amended to show a knowledge of the receiver's interests and priorities.

Applications for large-scale funds are more likely to succeed if they have the following characteristics:

1   Specificity. They should have a clear purpose and evidence of carefully planned procedures for achieving the proposed objective.

2   Originality. A cause will have more chance of success if it sets an example to others, and is likely to inspire future developments.

3   Urgency. It should be likely to have reasonably quick results

and solve a pressing problem, such as a need to incorporate more industry-based assignments into a technology course or provide community facilities in an inner-city area.

4   Newsworthiness. A project that is original or unusual has more obvious interest and appeal. For example, a major piece of equipment for use by handicapped children is likely to gain immediate sympathy. Evidence of existing support and publicity, such as newspaper reports, will also help a school's case. Ideally, the proposed project will help to maintain or establish the school's reputation for an aspect of its work such as overseas links, music, sport or community service.

5   A pump-priming role. A project that is likely to inspire future developments, such as a new style of course or a novel work experience scheme, is more attractive, especially if the school can demonstrate proof of potential support from the LEA or other sources once the scheme has been established. The supporting organization can thus provide initial funding to get a project going until it is self-supporting or funded by the government or other bodies.

6   Co-funding. For large-scale projects it is likely that the school will have to assemble a package of assistance from different sources. The amounts donated to individual schools by charities, firms and other organizations will rarely be more than a few hundred pounds. Most organizations prefer to co-fund with others rather than finance a project alone. Funding will generally be one-off or short-term, and the organization will want to be sure that the venture will be self-sustaining.

These factors can be turned to the school's benefit. If it can state to potential donors that 'such-and-such an organization has supported us', or that 'we have already raised x per cent of our target and only need £x', it will have an immediate advantage. Precise details of any firm support should therefore be given.

7   Quantifiable aims. The aims of the project should be clear and quantifiable wherever possible. Details of actual targets may not be required in an initial application, but should be available to clarify the purpose to both potential donors and the school itself.

Budgets

More ambitious projects will require a detailed forecast of likely costs. Circumstances will vary, but the breakdown might include:

1 capital costs – for example, vehicles, equipment;
2 running costs – for example, fuel, labour, materials;
3 allowances for inflation and unforeseen contingencies;
4 for long-term projects, a breakdown of costs and income over time; and
5 an allowance for hidden costs such as secretarial or teacher time.

Systems

A methodical administrative approach will be more cost-effective and create a better impression. It should be clear who is responsible for drafting, checking and signing appeals. Records should be kept of applications and their progress monitored. When donations or requests for further information are received they should be acknowledged promptly.

Charities and charitable trusts

Charities and charitable trusts may be willing to subsidize school-based projects. There is actually no legal distinction between charities and charitable trusts. As a rule of thumb, trusts give money to other organizations, and charities carry out their own work. However, some bodies fulfil both these functions. Schools, especially those in the state-maintained sector, rarely think of charities and charitable trusts as a source of assistance, but in certain circumstances charitable aid may be feasible.

Charities do not want to devote their limited income to financing projects that replace statutory provision. If, however, a school can demonstrate its ability to fulfil a relevant need, charitable support may be a realistic and legitimate source of funding. All charities have legal objects and policies that determine their support for particular causes. Typical causes that might be furthered by schools include support for the mentally and physically handicapped, performing arts, craft training and links with other countries.

Some trusts are restricted to helping pupils from a particular area, or pupils who have parents in particular occupations. Grants may be for individual pupils or teachers, or for projects that help a particular group of people.

Charities vary considerably in their policies and the amount that they can donate, so it is important to study them carefully, and consider how far their work and priorities are compatible with those of the school. A charity's priorities may change from year to year. Some trusts support different groups or individuals each year, and allocate money on an annual basis. Others commit their funds for several years ahead, leaving little or no money for new causes.

Other information that should be sought includes the following:

1 what type of project does the trust prefer to fund?
2 what will the trust refuse to fund?
3 does it prefer or insist upon co-funding?
4 are unsolicited applications welcomed, or even considered?
5 when do applications have to be made, and to whom?
6 what are the procedures for application?
7 what is the trust's annual grant expenditure?
8 what is the size of the average grant?

Much of this information is easily available in the standard reference books (Directory of Social Change 1991b), but it may sometimes be necessary to phone or write for more detail.

In addition to financial grants given by charitable trusts, it may be possible to obtain assistance for projects that are relevant to the aims of major charities. For example, a school that wished to provide a service to local pensioners or handicapped children might well obtain funding or professional advice from any of the charities in the particular field.

In recent years, charities have perceived increasing desperation in the applications submitted by schools, with requests for basic needs such as textbooks and teachers' salaries. In general, such applications have been unsuccessful, as charities see such provision as being the responsibility of the state. Appeals that have been successful have tended to be either particularly original or demonstrate the ability to provide services for the community. For example, an appeal to establish a community room for a council estate is likely to succeed where a simple request for extra classroom space is extremely unlikely to be supported.

Industry

Businesses give large amounts of time and money to schools every year, ranging from small gifts for fêtes to large-scale funding. There are many different forms of aid to schools and their pupils. The following list gives just a few examples:

1 money donations;
2 gifts of redundant equipment;
3 sponsorship of new equipment purchases;
4 raffle prizes;
5 professional help;
6 advertisements in the school magazine, yearbook or programme;
7 sponsorship of trophies; and
8 company grants for students on educational courses.

In approaching firms, the basic guidelines are very similar to those for applying to charitable trusts. Like charities, firms are very different in their approach to giving to schools. Some elementary research may be necessary. The best published source is the *Guide to Company Giving* (Directory of Social Change 1991a).

Policies of firms on charitable giving include the following:

1 never;
2 only when asked, with no particular priorities;
3 only to particular causes, often pet causes of directors or linked to the company's business;
4 concentrated in a geographical area;
5 large amounts to a few causes;
6 small amounts to many causes;
7 mainly to or through national charities, or their own charitable fund;
8 centralized at head office;
9 devolved to local branches; and
10 mainly to high-profile causes or events that attract publicity.

As can be seen, there is a tremendous variety of approaches. Firms are less likely than charities or government agencies to have clear criteria or administrative procedures for charitable giving, which may make them easier to approach. The corollary of this, however, is that it is often harder to predict a firm's attitude to a particular request for support.

If possible, requests should be linked to the firm's products:

help for a school farm might be obtained from an animal feed supplier or machinery may be sponsored by an engineering firm. Opportunism may also bring results. For example, a large firm moving into the school's area may be looking for good publicity, and may not have existing commitments.

There are no hard-and-fast rules about approaching firms, but some general rules apply.

1 Research the firm. What sort of help has it given in the past? Who decides which activities the firm will support? Does it already favour a particular school or area?
2 Personal contact is important. If the owner or a senior manager has a child at the school, there may be more chance of success.
3 Vague requests are seldom successful. The benefits of the project should be clearly stated without the use of jargon.

Usually, the first approaches should be made to local firms or local branches of national companies. Once a local contact has been established it may be worth approaching the head office if applicable. Local contacts may well support the application and supply useful information or contacts.

An approach need not necessarily be made to the management of a firm. In large firms workers often make donations through a social club or similar body. Even if there is no formal organization, one or two sympathetic workers might be able to convince their colleagues that the school's cause is worth supporting. This is particularly likely if a significant part of the work-force has links with the school as parents or past pupils.

Government

Large sums of money are issued every year in discretionary grants by central and local government and government agencies. These are in addition to statutory funding, and may be available to schools. There is no reason why, for example, a school providing facilities for the community should not obtain funding from community development programmes.

As with charitable trusts and industry, there are no hard-and-fast rules about obtaining this money. Generally, grants will tend to come from local rather than central government, although there are exceptions to this. This situation is changing with the development of LMS and the changes in local authority funding. The

basic rule is to 'ask around'. Again, careful research of the donor
agencies' priorities, regulations and administration is important.
Obtaining the support of council officers, councillors or MPs will
make success more probable. Two books that, although basically
aimed at voluntary groups, provide useful advice on approaching
local and central government and government agencies are *Raising
Money from Government* (Norton 1985) and *Opening the Town Hall
Door* (Hutt 1988).

CONCLUSION

The ideal fund-raising project would be one that raised a large
sum of money without making people aware that they were giving
up their time and cash. It would also be a positive experience for
pupils, staff and other organizers. Everybody would feel that they
had done something worthwhile, and would not resent the effort
and aggravation involved.

If this situation is to be possible it is important to consider how
a fund-raising campaign should be planned and whether it is likely
to be cost-effective. Managers should make a realistic appraisal of
the potential benefits and balance these against the resources –
monetary and non-monetary – that will have to be used in the
process.

External fund-raising should be seen as a way of developing the
curriculum rather than as a means of plugging gaps left by inadequate funding. It is unlikely that external fund-raising will compensate for inadequate government funding or privately paid fees.
Appeals that are positive and offer genuine extra benefits to pupils
and the local community are more likely to be attractive to potential fund providers.

Part 5

In conclusion

Chapter 16

External relations and the future

Tim Brighouse

To reflect the advance of the 'market', educational libraries will soon be full of books on 'marketing in education': in the same way, the past twenty years have witnessed a growth of books on evaluation in the wake of accountability debates. Already, at the beginning of 1992 in the UK, two universities and one polytechnic are running Masters courses in business administration, directly targeted at the educational market. (It will be noted that even the language we use is redolent with the subliminal messages we wish to convey.)

In my childhood, shops had customers, solicitors clients, British Railways (sic) passengers and schools pupils. Of course, distance lends simplicity and enchantment to days when rationing was seen as a fair way to share out resources amid post-war shortages and when consumerism was but a gleam in J. Walter Thompson's eye.

The post-war consensus about the appropriate role of the state and the individual was perhaps best encapsulated by the word Butskellism, but this evaporated slowly in the wake of increasing affluence and disintegrated altogether after the oil crisis of the early 1970s. Neither education nor the rest of the public services could continue to absorb such a high proportion of the gross domestic product of a declining industrial nation. The economic decline and pressure lent an acerbic urgency to the questioning of the efficacy of schooling that seems to be a perennial feature of education systems, at least in North America and Great Britain. Moreover, ameliorating the worst effects of increasing unemployment and making provision for old age became rivals for what public money there was and together began to make far greater demands on the gross domestic product, to the disadvantage of education. Questioning the state's capacity to deliver the post-war dream about public services has not been confined to education: most informed commentators, for example, believe that a National Health Service is simply not affordable. Eleven years of Thatcherism therefore ushered into the schooling system a stream of ideas that had seemed unthinkable when they first surfaced in the late 1960s.

Those who had the vision to see the inevitability of such events anticipated them, and in so doing may have unwittingly reinforced their progress. For example, after living through the consequences of the William Tyndale affair in London and having worked with the Council of Local Education Authorities and the Association of County Councils, I did not need to be a genius, nor to have acquired the gift of second sight, to diagnose 'accountability' as the key issue for the education service when I was appointed chief education officer in Oxfordshire in 1978. Indeed, my new employers had been the first to decide – although, thanks to my determined prevarication, not the first to act on the decision – to publish examination results 'in order that parents might make a better choice of school' in the three months preceding my appointment in that year.

It seemed to me then, and it still does, that if one could anticipate events it would be possible to shape them ever so slightly in changed directions: so it was that Oxfordshire asked schools to take part in the country's first externally required schools' self-evaluation exercise. 'If governors, parents and county councillors knew more of what actually happened in schools', I argued to the staff and headteachers, 'perhaps elected politicians – and the public they claimed to understand so well through their doorstep activities in being elected – would eventually support more investment and confidence in schools as they got to know more about them'. Perhaps some instinct guided us towards this particularly benevolent form of accountability, for, of course, collective self-review leading to development plans is one of the seven key processes that are linked to school effectiveness. (Brighouse and Tomlinson 1990).

It was a vain attempt as events turned out, swept away by the encroaching tide that has applied market principles to the running of the education service. In pessimistic moments one views the logical outcome as a bewildering bazaar with noisy schools advertising their wares as they follow the prevailing fashions of consumerism, each recognizing the accountability only of the market.

If, however, we take a more measured view and are to begin to understand and predict the future external role of the leaders of schools, it is perhaps best to understand the main strands that have created the present. The headings of the chapters of this book bear testimony to the changed landscape.

There are seven main strands that have increased the importance of the schools' external role. First, the collapse of the consensus to which I referred earlier led to increased calls for accountability, with a sub-text of debate about parents' (and others') rights rather than their responsibilities. Second, the speed of change demanded that the curriculum change with more frequency to keep pace with the advance in knowledge. Third, politicians became more than usually impatient with the length of time it seemed to take schools to respond to the needs of change, so they did not merely enter the secret garden of the curriculum but became keen cultivators of it themselves (Judge 1988). Fourth, the decade or more of falling rolls required that those people external to schools but responsible for their planning – the local authorities and national government – interrupted the closed and secure nature of the work of the schools in order to force a closure here or an amalgamation there. (The management of contraction is a much more disturbing process than the management of expansion.)

Fifth, following the 1987 election, the Conservative government began to apply to education the market principles it had earlier applied to the major economic practices of a nation. The lessons of Milton Friedman were applied to the provision of education and other public services, just as they had been applied to the economy: indeed, the government was prompted to do so through observing the example of the World Bank, which specifically tied the application of free market principles to the running of public services in South American and other under-developed countries as a condition of aid. Sixth, a comparative decline in the economic well-being of the country, as reflected through GDP, has meant that a schooling system starved of cash has begun to rely to an increasing extent on charitable and private finance, and less direct sources of public finance. (The occasional school fête for a minibus is now sometimes supported by major sponsorship, covenanted giving and charitable status, accounting for a far greater part of the school budget.)

Seventh, there has inevitably been a growth of voluntarism with the decline of the influence of the central state. That voluntarism affects schools in many ways: adults other than teachers may offer their services as helpers in the classroom or sometimes as supplementary educators, or as the organizers of pupils themselves, either in the main curriculum as reciprocating volunteers, giving services to those in the local community less fortunate than themselves, or in a wider curriculum as raisers of money for deserving causes. These can either be on a one-off basis or perennially to the great new charitable organizations such as Children in Need, Telethon or Comic Relief. The irony of the last factor was brought home to me with unusual clarity when a school I know prided itself on the amount it had raised for Telethon one spring and stretched out its hand to the same agency for an adventure playground the following autumn.

Which of these factors that combined to make the external agenda of the school have almost run their course? Which have more to run, and how will or can they be affected? Are there others in prospect that will replace them? Some answers are obvious. The factors that are connected with demography have in general run their course. There will always be areas where school populations rise and fall, and to some extent, the introduction of market choice will create more violent swings of school populations, at least in areas where a surplus exists or where the technology schools are built to create a surplus.

Those factors driven by educational considerations will behave after the fashion of all fashions. Some are timeless and as old as Socrates; others will flicker briefly and disappear; still others will gain more or less emphasis but remain a part of the scene; and, finally, a few represent a departure in our trade or profession. Into the latter category probably come information technology (IT) and all the microprocessor-driven changes to the skills of teaching and learning that call for all to be alert to the need to update. In short, staff development is a function with external implications.

So too, importantly, is the new-found multi-faceted role of parents. It is not simply their role as captive supporters, nor as consumers, nor as governors, nor even as shareholders within the governors' annual meeting that the school has to consider. It is also their potential as joint educators. In all roles, in any case, they need to be informed and, most important of all, informed about the education of their child. Chapter 8 has emphasized that role. This potential is comparatively unexplored in most of our schools. It is only twenty years ago that 'no parents beyond this point' signs were being removed from London schools, many of which had broken glass embedded in their fortress-like school perimeter walls.

It is those factors driven by socio-economic and political pressures that are the hardest to predict. It could be that trust in the market is so great that, like parental involvement, it is an irreversible trend. Nevertheless, it seems likely that the excesses of the application of market forces will soon lead to some substantial review of the mechanisms designed to underpin it. In particular, it seems at least possible that the sudden escalation in the number of children excluded from school for behavioural reasons (and the growth in the number of such pupils in special schools and units) – fuelled by the present system of formula funding within the local management of schools – will produce unfairness of such a gross nature that modifications will be introduced. Perhaps programmes of 'positive action' will emerge within at least some local education authorities that focus more clearly on the development of quality and content than quantity and provision, as was the case at the time of the ill-fated EPA programme. The Chilean experience in Pinochet's last years shows that even right-wing governments can be shamed into action programmes directed at areas of great disadvantage. Perhaps the mixed economy of public and private finances is as given; it certainly seems so if one observes the retreat from 'statism' that is implied in the policies and statements of politicians of the right, left and centre. In short most of the socio-economic and political pressures will remain, intensified by yet greater acceleration in knowledge (and the speed of communicating that knowledge), but also accompanied by some moderation in market principles. 'Non-stop' change, however, is inevitable.

What all this adds up to is a substantial external agenda for the leaders of our schools to handle. The role of headteacher has become infinitely more complex than it was as recently as the 1980s, and certainly compared to the role of those who practised the profession a decade or so earlier. In their day, the stars were fixed in the heavens, the seasons could be relied upon (and even punctuated the school curriculum), the divorce rate was ten times lower than it is today and the community bobby was on his bike. You could not only believe that the sun would rise in the east but you could even behave as though it did. The timetable lasted from one year to the next. The general public's view of schools in those days was as strange places. They were the equivalent of islands where strange people – teachers – who were much respected were the equivalent of witch doctors and carried out unseen initiation rites. The young of the tribe magically emerged at the end of their difficult teenage years as adults with a greater or lesser degree of skill, confidence and competence for life as working citizens. Indeed, their working lives would be spent in an occupation that would never change. To some extent this model is still to be seen in the private and independent sector of schooling.

Those days are long gone in the public sector of schooling. The school is a public place, required to interact with all the agencies and in all the ways that this book has documented. Moreover, the 'marketplace' school is not merely public; many of those who interact with it and who are described in this book claim to have a stake in its direction and purposes. Many of their particular agenda, never mind their priorities, are mutually incompatible – with each other and with those of the school.

Change, therefore, is the key issue facing those in the market and in the school. It has become a way of life. Change comes in three broad categories: internally generated; externally available; and externally required. The passage of the various Acts of Parliament throughout the 1980s has ensured that the externally required category of change has been a regular and recent phenomenon for school managers. It poses challenges quite unlike the other two because it intrudes on and affects the pace of the school's internal agenda of self-selected change. Moreover, some of the changes will not fit in with the school's internal value system or its essential next phase of development, while other parts are so badly designed, notwithstanding the apparent external imperative, that the wise school headteacher and staff will quietly bide their time until a more considered view emerges from public deliberations. So it is turning out with the National Curriculum, with many schools waiting for the next revision before embarking on work that they see as likely to be abortive. Headteachers have to judge not only which externally required change they are going to take a risk on and ignore, but also which they can delay and which can be harnessed to an internal imperative and priority. They need to recognize the important distinction between changes that affect information or ideas, which are relatively easy to handle, of course, and changes that affect skills and attitudes, which are infinitely more difficult. They need to be wary of the danger to staff morale of fiddling with incentive allowances (after all, one person's incentive allowance may prove a disincentive to a dozen others). They will be familiar with the infinite capacity of teachers to adopt materials to disguise the lack of real change in classroom techniques; they will consider whether change in the curriculum also requires change in management and organization; and they will be alert to the need to show their own personal interest in the change they support.

That brings us to the heart of the external role: the need to keep the various constituents and priorities both inside and outside the school in balance. Many leaders have lost their internal grip by becoming enchanted and preoccupied with the external. At a time of great externally inspired change – and there is no prospect that the future will bring any lessening of the onslaught – the external agenda is much larger and demands the most skilful handling.

All those responsible for running an organization have legitimate 'constituencies' – or interest groups – that have a greater or lesser claim on their attention. The larger the organization, the greater the number both of categories of constituency and of people within each category. For example, the teacher in the classroom has the children he or she teaches, the teaching colleagues whom they may lead or be led by, including the headteacher, other staff and, of course, the parents of the children whom they teach every day. The headteacher, on the other hand, has all the teachers, all the staff, all the parents and, if less directly, all the children; the headteacher has, too, the governors, the LEA in its various mani- festations, the local community, other headteachers, local com- munity interests and, perhaps, the local college that provides stu- dents for training, as well as partner primary/secondary schools and people from the multitude of agencies with which the school must deal for children's individual needs and the school's collective needs. How people divide their time between these interest groups will affect how they do their job and, sometimes a different matter, how they are perceived to do their job.

This chapter has attempted to show how the context within which education is practised has changed dramatically and to some extent with increasing unpredictability as it is exposed to market forces and the increasing speed of change in other walks of life. The successful leader is able to judge what time to give to each constituency with a legitimate claim on his or her time and even individuals within each constituency. So the headteacher

1952	1992	2002
LEA****	LEA**	?
PARENTS	PARENTS****	
GOVERNORS*	GOVERNORS***	?
TEACHERS****	TEACHERS****	
OTHER STAFF****	OTHER STAFF***	?
INDUSTRY/ COMMERCE	INDUSTRY/ COMMERCE***	?
PROFESSIONAL BODIES	PROFESSIONAL BODIES*	?
OTHER AGENCIES*	OTHER AGENCIES***	
PRESS	PRESS***	
LOCAL COMMUNITY*	LOCAL COMMUNITY**	

Number of asterisks indicates intensity

Figure 16.1 Main interest groups with claims on headteacher's time

knows instinctively how to engage a key figure within the staffroom in casual conversation in order to defuse a tricky situation in an upcoming meeting; or, in less Machiavellian style, knows when a particular teacher needs a classroom visit and personal praise or a warm personal note of thanks. My illustrations are deliberately from an internal, not an external, constituency.

Figure 16.1 sets out a purely illustrative list of interest groups or constituencies that a headteacher might have had to deal with forty years ago and those they deal with today. The number has grown and their respective importance has changed. The third column in the table is for the reader to fill in. If LEAs are retained and have some powers of planning returned to them – of proposing and disposing – the day may yet return when the wise headteacher sees the LEA as an important courtier of his or her time. If however, LEAs become merely regulators they will need less attention and of a different kind.

So it will be with all the potential interest groups. One thing will be the same in the future as in the past – namely, that success

both for the leader and the school will come to those with the
sensitivity, perception and judgement to give the correct amount of
attention to each legitimate interest group as the context demands,
always remembering that if they neglect teaching, learning and
children, their external profile, however impressive superficially,
will simply be a facade.

Appendix

USEFUL CONTACTS IN INDUSTRY

The number of organizations involved in links between schools and industry is enormous – almost too many to list. Schools seeking help in developing partnerships with local industry will find that there are many sources of such help, at all levels and of all types.

Contact

Aims and areas of interest

School Curriculum Industry Partnership (SCIP) University of Warwick Centre for Education in Industry Coventry CV4 7AL Tel: 0203 523954

Introducing into the education of young people an awareness and understanding of industry in the industrial society in which we live. SCIP has regional co-ordinators who are able to develop work locally with schools and LEAs.

Science and Technology Regional Organization (SATRO) SATRO National Co-ordinator 76 Portland Place London W1N 4AA Tel: 071–278–2468

Enhancing the understanding of science, technology, engineering and industry among young people. Providing teaching resources with an industrial emphasis. Promoting industry-related problem-solving work in schools.
The SATRO network is regional and involves key people from schools, industry and LEAs. In many areas the SATRO carries out activities with other link organizations.

Understanding British Industry (UBI) UBI Headquarters Sun Alliance House New Inn Hall Street Oxford OX1 2QE Tel: 0865 722585

Improving the understanding of industry and commerce among teachers, as well as working to improve the understanding of the education system in business.

Trident Trust 91 Brick Lane London E1 6QN Tel: 071–375 0245

Project Trident works for the personal development of young people in full-time education through schemes that involve work placement and involvement in the local community.

Young Enterprise Ewert Place Summertown Oxford OX2 7BZ Tel: 0865 311180

Providing practical opportunities for young people at school to run an industrial enterprise or model company.

Understanding Industry 91 Waterloo Road London SE1 8XP Tel: 071–620 0735

Putting business managers into schools and colleges to talk to 16–19-year-old students as part of the school curriculum, and generally getting businesses working with local schools.

Confederation of British Industry (CBI) Centre Point 103 New Oxford Street London WC1A 1DU Tel: 071–379 7400

Encouraging schemes that will bring about a closer understanding between education and industry, working through its own full-time central education department.

References

Audit Commission (1989a) *Losing an Empire; Finding a Role – the LEA in the Future*, Audit Commission Occasional Papers Number 10, London: HMSO.

Audit Commission (1989b) *Assuring Quality in Education: The Role of Local Education Authority Inspectors and Advisers*, London: HMSO.

Ballinger, E. (1986) 'The training and development needs of managers: an overview', in C. Day and R. Moore (eds) *Staff Development in the Secondary School – Management Perspectives*, London: Croom Helm.

Barnett, C. (1979) 'Technology, education and industrial and economic strength', *Journal of the Royal Society 5, 271, 127: 32–40*.

Bolton, E. (1991) 'Charter bears a closer inspection', *Times Educational Supplement* 3929: 10–11.

Brighouse, T. and Tomlinson, J. (1990) *Successful Schools*, London: IPPR.

Brown, R. (1987) *Marketing for the Small Firm*, London: Cassell.

Bryce Report (1895) *Report of the Royal Commission on Secondary Education*, London: HMSO.

Bush, T. (1986) *Theories of Educational Management*, London: Harper & Row.

Bush, T. (1988) 'Action and theory in school management – E325', in *Managing Schools*, Milton Keynes: The Open University.

Cave, E. and Demick, D. (1990) 'Marketing the school', in E. Cave and C. Wilkinson (eds) (1990) *Local Management of Schools: Some Practical Issues*, London: Routledge.

Cave, E. and Wilkinson, C. (eds) (1990) *Local Management of Schools: Some Practical Issues*, London: Routledge.

Charities Aid Foundation (1991) *Directory of Grant-Making Trusts*, 12th edn, London: Charities Aid Foundation.

Clough, A. H. (1896) 'The Bothie of Tober-na-Vuolich', in F. L. Mulhauser (ed.) (1974) *Poems of Arthur Hugh Clough*, 2nd edn, Oxford: Clarendon Press.

Coulson, A. (1985) *The Managerial Behaviour of Primary School Heads*, Abingdon: Carfax Publishing Company.

Crowther Report (1959) *15–18*, Central Advisory Council for Education, London: HMSO.

Davies, H. (1991) 'Put the people first', *Times Educational Supplement* 3918:7.

Davies, P. and Scribbins, K. (1985) *Marketing Further and Higher Education*, London: Longman for Further Education Unit.

Day, C. (1986) 'Staff development: some problems in promoting professional learning and change', in C. Day and R. Moore (eds) *Staff Development in the Secondary School – Management Perspectives*, London: Croom Helm.

Department of Education and Science (1965) *The Organisation of Secondary Education*, Circular 10/65, London: HMSO.

Department of Education and Science (1972) *Teacher Education and Training*, report of the James Committee, London: HMSO.

Department of Education and Science (1988a) *Advancing A-levels*, report of the Higginson Committee, London: HMSO.

Department of Education and Science (1988b) *Local Management of Schools*, circular 7/88, London: HMSO.

Department of Education and Science (1989) *Initial Teacher Training*, circular 10/89, London: HMSO.

Department of Education and Science (1991a) *School Governors – the School Curriculum*, London: HMSO.

Department of Education and Science (1991b) *Education and Training for the 21st Century*, White Paper, Cmnd 1536, London: HMSO.

Department of Education and Science (1992) *Reform of Initial Teacher Training – A Consultation Document*, London: HMSO.

Devlin, T. and Knight, B. (1990) *Public Relations and Marketing in Schools*, London: Longman.

Directory of Social Change (1991a) *A Guide to Company Giving*, 4th edn, London: Directory of Social Change.

Directory of Social Change (1991b) *A Guide to The Major Grant Making Trusts*, 3rd edn, London: Directory of Social Change.

Directory of Social Change (1991c) *The Educational Grants Directory*, 2nd edn, London: Directory of Social Change.

Duffy, M. (1990) 'The changing relationship between schools and higher education', in G. Parry and C. Wake (eds) *Access and Alternative Futures for Higher Education*, London: Hodder & Stoughton.

Drucker, P. (1973) *Management tasks, responsibilities and practice*, London: Harper Row.

East Sussex County Council/University of Sussex (1979) *Accountability in the Middle Years of Schooling*, Lewes: East Sussex County Council.

Education Act 1944, London: HMSO.

Education Act 1980, London: HMSO.

Education (School Information) Regulations 1981, London: HMSO.

Education Reform Act 1988, London: HMSO.

Education (School Records) Regulations 1989, London: HMSO.

Education (School Curriculum and Related Information) Regulations 1989, London: HMSO.

Education (Individual Pupils' Achievements) (Information) Regulations 1990, London: HMSO.

Fallon, M. (1991) 'Goodbye to all that: the Fallon interview', *Managing Schools Today* 1, 1:3–8.

Forster, P. and Ives, M. (1990) *Promoting Your School: A Practical Guide to Promotion and Public Relations for Schools*, Harrogate: School Marketing.

Foskett, N. H. (1988) 'Planning schools' liaison activities in departments', unpublished report, Aston University Schools' Liaison Office.

Foskett, N. H. (1991) 'A survey of school responses to hosting PGCE students', unpublished report, School of Education, University of Southampton.

Foskett, N. H. and Foskett, R. (1989) 'Geography and higher education: a potential applicant's guide', *Geography Review* 4, 3:39–41.

Fullan, M. (1991) *The New Meaning of Educational Change*, London: Routledge.

Glatter, R. (ed.) (1989) *Educational Institutions and their Environments: Managing the Boundaries*, Milton Keynes: Open University Press.

Gleeson, D. (ed.) (1989) *TVEI and Secondary Education: A Critical Appraisal*, London: Open University Press.

Gorman, G. (1988) *Fund Raising for Schools*, London: Kogan Page.

Gorman, G. (1989) *School–Industry Links*, London: Kogan Page.

Gray, L. (1989) 'Marketing educational services', in R. Glatter, (ed.) *Educational Institutions and their Environments: Managing the Boundaries*, Milton Keynes: Open University Press.

Gray, L. (1991) *Marketing Education*, London: Open University Press.

Handy, C. (1989) *The Age of Unreason*, London: Hutchinson.

Hanford, I. (1990) 'Secondary school image', *Management in Education* 4, 3:142–8.

Hargreaves, D. H., Hopkins, D., Leask, M., Connolly, J. and Robinson, P. (1989) *Planning for School Development*, London: HMSO.

Heap, B. (1990) *Degree Course Offers 1990*, London: Careers Consultants Ltd.

HMI (1988) *The New Teacher in School*, London: HMSO.

Holmes, G. (1977) *The Idiot Teacher*, London: Spokesman Press.

Hoy, W. K. and Miskel, C. G. (1989) 'Schools and their external environments', in R. Glatter (ed.) *Educational Institutions and their Environments: Managing the Boundaries*, Milton Keynes: Open University Press.

Hutt, J. (1988) *Opening the Town Hall Door*, London: Bedford Square Press.

Johnson, D. and Ransom, E. (1983) *Family and School*, London: Croom Helm.

Judge, H. (1988) *A Generation of Schooling*, Oxford: Oxford University Press.

Keen, C. and Greenall, J. (1987) *Public Relations Management in Colleges, Polytechnics and Universities*, Banbury: HEIST Publications.

Keen, C. and Higgins, T. (1990) *Young People's Knowledge of Higher Education*, Banbury: HEIST/PCAS.

Keen, C. and Warner, D. (eds) (1989) *Visual and Corporate Identity*, Banbury: HEIST Publications.

MacBeth, A. (1989) *Involving Parents – Effective Parent–Teacher Relations*, Oxford: Heinemann.

Maden, M. (1991) *Times Educational Supplement* 3929:3.

Marsden, C. (1991) *Education and Business – A Vision for the Partnership*, London: BP Educational Service.

Megson, C. and Baber, M. (1986) *Taking Education Further: A Practical Guide to College Marketing Success*, Stratford-upon-Avon: MSE Publications.

Ministry of Education (1947) *The New Secondary Education*, pamphlet 9, London: HMSO.

Ministry of Education (1963) *Report of the Committee of Enquiry Chaired by Lord Robbins*, London: HMSO.

Mintzberg, H. (1979) *The Structuring of Organisations*, Englewood Cliffs, N.J.: Prentice Hall.

Mountfield, A. (1991) *State Schools: A Suitable Case for Charity?*, London: Directory of Social Change.

National Association of Head Teachers (1990) *The Marketing of Schools*, London: NAHT.

National Consumer Council (1977) *Question Marks for Schools*, London: National Consumer Council.

National Consumer Council (1986a) *Annual Report for 1985–6*, London: National Consumer Council.

National Consumer Council (1986b) *The Missing Links Between Home and School*, London: National Consumer Council.

National Curriculum Council (1990a) *The Whole Curriculum: Curriculum Guidance 3*, York: National Curriculum Council.

National Curriculum Council (1990b) *Education for Economic and Industrial Understanding*, York: National Curriculum Council.

National Curriculum Council (1991) *Education for Citizenship: Curriculum Guidance 8*, York: National Curriculum Council.

Naybour, S. (1989) 'Parents: partners or customers?', in J. Sayer and V. Williams (eds) *Schools and External Relations: Managing the New Partnerships*, London: Cassell Education.

Norton, M. (1985) *Raising Money from Government*, 2nd edn, London: Directory of Social Change.

Norton, M. (1988) *A Guide to the Benefits of Charitable Status*, 2nd edn, London: Directory of Social Change.

Norton, M. (1991) *Raising Money from Industry*, 2nd edn, London: Directory of Social Change.

Nottingham University School of Education (1978) *Communication Between Home and School*, Nottingham: Nottingham University.

O'Connor, M. (1990) *Managing Communications*, London: Secondary Heads Association.

Olins, W. (1989) *Corporate Identity*, London: Thames & Hudson.

Parry, G. (1989) *Access and Preparatory Courses Offered by or in Association with the Universities – A Report on a Survey undertaken by SCUE*, London: CVCP.

Parry, G. and Wake, C. (1990) *Access and Alternative Futures for Higher Education*, London: Hodder & Stoughton.

Pascal, C. (1989) 'Democratized primary school government: conflicts and dichotomies', in R. Glatter (ed.) *Educational Institutions and their Environments: Managing the Boundaries*, Milton Keynes: Open University Press.

Perry, P. (1991) 'A view from Quality Street', *Times Educational Supplement* 3911:5.

Peters, T. J. and Waterman, R. H. (1982) *In Search of Excellence*, New York: Harper Row.

Phillips, A. (1988) *Charitable Status: A Practical Handbook*, 3rd edn, London: Interchange Books.

Pike, A. (1991) 'External relations at Henry Harbin School, Poole', unpublished MA research, School of Education, University of Southampton.

Playfair, L. (1855) 'The study of abstract science essential to the progress of industry', introductory lecture at the Government School of Mines, session 1851–2, printed in *British Eloquence: lectures and addresses*, London. Reprinted in Roderick, G. W. and Stephens, M. D. (1978) *Education and Industry in the Nineteenth Century*, London: Longman.

Rée, H. (1973) *Educator Extraordinary: the life and achievement of Henry Morris*, London: Longman.

Roberts, D. and Higgins, T. (1992) *Higher Education. The Student Experience*, Leeds: HEIST Publications.

Royal Society of Arts (1986) *Industry Year*, publicity leaflet, London: Royal Society of Arts.

Sallis, J. (1988) *Schools, Parents and Governors – A New Approach to Accountability*, London: Routledge.

Sams, B. (1991) 'Minister, let's be friends', *Times Educational Supplement* 3917:22.

Sayer, J. (1989) 'The public context of change', in J. Sayer and V. Williams (eds) *Schools and External Relations: Managing the New Partnerships*, London: Cassell Education.

Sayer, J. and Williams, V. (eds) (1989) *Schools and External Relations: Managing the New Partnerships*, London: Cassell Education.

School Management Task Force (1989) *Developing School Management: The Way Forward*, London: HMSO.

Schools Council (1973) *16–19: Growth and Response*, Schools Council working paper 46.

Schools Examination and Assessment Council (1990) *Examinations Post–16: Developments for the 1990s*, London: SEAC.

Sexton, S. (1990) 'Free market's better values', *Times Educational Supplement* 3868:20.

Shattock, M. and Walker, P. (1977) 'The factors influencing student choice of university', *Research in Education* 18:67–74.

Skrimshire, A. (1981) 'Community schools and the end of the "Social" individual', *Oxford Review of Education* 7, 1:53–66.

Smith, P. (1991) 'A sharp rise in child benefit', *Times Educational Supplement* 3928:8.

Spurgeon, M. (1987) *Fund Raising Without Fail*, London: Elliot Right Way Books.

Stillman, A. and Grant, M. (1989) *The LEA Adviser – A Changing Role*, London: NFER–Nelson.

Stigler, G. S. (1963) *The Intellectual and the Market Place*, occasional paper No. 5, London: Institute of Economic Affairs.

Tilling, M. (1988) *Press and Public Relations in Education: A Practical Guide*, Sheffield papers in education management 75, Sheffield City Polytechnic.

Torrington, D. and Weightman, J. (1989) *The Reality of School Management*, Oxford: Basil Blackwell.

Tough, A. (1988) *Why Adults Learn: a study of the major reasons for beginning and continuing a learning project*, Toronto: Ontario Institute for Studies in Education.

Toyne, P. (1990) 'Achieving wider access', in G. Parry and C. Wake (eds) *Access and Alternative Futures for Higher Education*, London: Hodder & Stoughton.

Tuckett, A. (1990) 'A higher education system fit for adult learners', in G. Parry and C. Wake (eds) *Access and Alternative Futures for Higher Education*, London: Hodder & Stoughton.

Wake, C. (1989) 'AS levels and the universities', in J. Hughes (ed.) *AS levels: Implications for Schools, Examining Boards and Universities*, London: Falmer Press.

Wallis, J. and Mee, G. (1983) *Community Schools – Claims and Performance*, Nottingham: University of Nottingham Department of Adult Education.

Watts, J. (1980) *Towards an Open School*, London: Longman.

Weindling, D. and Earley, P. (1987) *Secondary Headship: The First Years*, London: NFER–Nelson.

Williams, V. (1989) 'Schools and their communities: issues in external relations', in J. Sayer and V. Williams (eds) *Schools and External Relations: Managing the New Partnerships*, London: Cassell Education.

Index